CANADIAN HAUNTINGS

TRUE GHOST STORIES

Adapted from *Haunted America* and *Historic Haunted America*

by
Michael Norman
and
Beth Scott

SCHOLASTIC CANADA LTD.
Toronto New York London Auckland Sydney
Mexico City New Delhi Hong Kong Buenos Aires

Scholastic Canada Ltd.
175 Hillmount Road, Markham, Ontario L6C 1Z7, Canada

Scholastic Inc.
555 Broadway, New York, NY 10012, USA

Scholastic Australia Pty Limited
PO Box 579, Gosford, NSW 2250, Australia

Scholastic New Zealand Limited
Private Bag 94407, Greenmount, Auckland, New Zealand

Scholastic Ltd.
Villiers House, Clarendon Avenue, Leamington Spa,
Warwickshire CV32 5PR, UK

Library and Archives Canada Cataloguing in Publication

Norman, Michael, 1947 June 29-
Canadian hauntings / Michael Norman and Beth Scott.

Stories selected from Haunted America, and Historic haunted America.

ISBN 0-439-95709-5

1. Haunted places--Canada. 2. Ghosts--Canada. I. Scott, Beth, 1922-
II. Norman, Michael, 1947 June 29- . Haunted America.
III. Norman, Michael, 1947 June 29- . Historic haunted. IV. Title.

BF1472.C3N67 2004   133.1'0971   C2004-904412-5

Interior illustration by Andrej Krystoforski
Cover copyright Masterfile/Zefa Photex/T Brummett House

The stories in this book were previously published in *Haunted America* and
Historic Haunted America. Published by arrangement with Tom Doherty
Associates, LLC.

6 5 4 3 2 1   Printed in Canada   04 05 06 07 08

TABLE OF CONTENTS

THE PORTRAIT

Chilliwack, British Columbia

In December 1965, artist Teresa Montgomery and her husband, Charles, moved into a stately twelve-room house in the Fraser Valley community of Chilliwack. Although the place had been used at one time as a boardinghouse, few major repairs were necessary. Cosmetic improvements alone would certainly go far in restoring the house to its earlier grandeur. The couple were fortunate to have found a house with such potential, and at a reasonable price, no less.

The story of what transpired in the Montgomerys' house was one of the most widely reported ghost stories in the British Columbia press of the 1960s. This is what happened to these surprised homeowners.

One afternoon while Teresa worked in the kitchen, she heard drawers opening and closing in an upstairs room. She was alone in the house. Dashing up the stairway, she threw open the doors to all the rooms. In an unused bedroom, she found an old chest that had come with the house, looking as if it had been ransacked; some drawers were partly open, and others were opened wide and jarred off their tracks. An iron bedstead, also left behind by the previous owners, sat in the middle of the floor. Teresa recalled seeing it against one wall on the day they'd moved in. The chest and the bed were the only furniture in the room.

Teresa didn't tell her husband, but as the days passed she became increasingly nervous in the huge house. Then came the frightening dreams in which she saw a woman lying on the hallway floor. The figure wore a red dress with a pattern of yellow flowers. "She is terrified," Teresa told a reporter.

The nightmares were making her ill. When her husband asked what was the matter, she said she must have become overly tired by the move. She continued to unpack trunks and boxes, arrange furniture, and hang pictures, but took little pleasure in the work. She cooked meals for Charles, but ate sparingly herself. Her husband wasn't overly concerned. He had lived long enough with his wife to recognize the artist's moods. He assumed she had been hard at work on some paintings, and on those occasions little else mattered. She disliked talking about her work, so Charles never asked.

Then, one morning in her studio, Teresa sat down at her easel to paint a portrait of the woman she'd seen in her dreams. Perhaps in this way she could rid herself of the ghastly dream. But something took control of the brush in her hand. Although she tried to paint the portrait of a woman, the face became that of a man — a man with strong, dark, virile features.

Nothing like this had ever happened to the artist before. Was she losing her talent? Her mind? Fright drove her from the studio that afternoon.

The next day Teresa found the portrait she'd left on the easel had changed. The man's dark eyes had become menacing, and deep shadows concealed one side of his face. Each morning thereafter Teresa would find the portrait altered in some way. She knew then that she would never be able to paint again, at least not in *this* house.

Then late one night a slight noise sent Teresa again into the unused bedroom. As she peered through the door, a dim light appeared in a window and in the centre of the light she glimpsed a woman's face. Although the features were somewhat indistinct, Teresa felt certain that this was the woman in her nightmares. This was the ghost who haunted her house.

Soon after the actual sighting of the mysterious woman, other phenomena developed. The front door began to open and close by itself. Footfalls were heard on the stairs when no one was there, and sounds of heavy breathing came from empty rooms.

As Teresa became acquainted with her neighbours, they told her tales about her house — perhaps more than she wanted to hear. One account had it that a woman had been murdered in the house and her body cremated in the chimney. Another story was of a man who'd committed suicide in the house a decade earlier. He was said to have occupied the empty room. The worried homeowner wondered if that might account for the heavy breathing she had heard. No one seemed to know if there'd been any connection between the two people, or, indeed, if either story had any basis in fact.

However, the previous owners, Rebecca and Jackson Perkins, told the Montgomerys that an old man living in the house *had* committed suicide, but he'd drowned himself in a slough behind the house. Mr. and Mrs. Perkins noted that they'd experienced nothing unusual during the four years they had lived in the house, and dismissed the rumours of ghost business as "baloney."

By spring the media got wind of the strange goings-on in Chilliwack. Teresa eagerly accepted all requests by reporters and photographers to tour the house, and she took special pains to show them the 1.2 by 1.8 metre portrait that she claimed was changing daily. She said the dark side of the picture had lightened, the outline of a cheek appeared, and a thin moustache was now visible.

One night during the last week of May 1966, Jess Odam, a staff reporter for the *Vancouver Sun,* and Ken Oakes, a *Sun* photographer, visited the house. They kept vigil in the unused bedroom, which was lit by one candle on the chest. A friend of Teresa Montgomery who did not wish to be identified sat with the two men. Teresa was in the kitchen preparing sandwiches.

At 12:25 A.M., Odam reported that he thought he heard a footstep out in the hallway. The friend said she'd heard a "sliding sound." Oakes, seated farthest from the doorway, heard nothing.

Moments later when Teresa came up the stairs with the tray of sandwiches, she discovered a piece of linoleum lying on the hallway floor. She took it into the room and showed her guests the place where it had been tacked to the wall. She'd seen it there on the day she and her husband had moved in and was certain that it was in place when the little group arrived.

Odam wrote, "We saw no ghost, we heard no ghost . . . or did we?"

The following week, at Teresa's request, Odam returned to the house to investigate a small turret at the corner of the building. Teresa had dreamed that the ghost lady "lived" in there. Perhaps the turret held a clue as to the woman's identity and her fate. Before Odam reached the house, Teresa had already broken an opening into the turret by removing some attic panelling. But fearing spiders, she dared not go in.

Odam armed himself with a flashlight and squeezed into the tiny space. Lying on his stomach, he swung the flashlight slowly in all directions. Nothing. Nothing but insulation material that had crumbled over the years and now littered the small floor. When Teresa saw it she said it looked similar to the white specks she'd seen in her dreams.

Shortly after Odam's visit, a former occupant telephoned the Montgomerys to report that there were secret chutes running from the top of the house to the bottom. For what purpose, the caller did not know. Teresa suspected it was a prank call, but there were so many questions without answers that she scheduled a séance.

A hypnotist and a clairvoyant met at the house on an afternoon in June. Teresa had moved a table and chairs into the empty bedroom. As the men seated themselves, she pulled down the room-darkening shades at the windows and lit a candle in the centre of the table. Charles Montgomery was posted in the front yard to keep sightseers away. (The newspaper articles had attracted some unwanted attention.)

"Is there anyone here?" asked the clairvoyant. "You may come forth now, please."

Silence.

The clairvoyant raised his voice. "We are here only to help you."

Teresa stared so intently at the candle that she saw multiple images of the flame.

"Do not fear us," said the hypnotist. "We bring you no

harm." There were no sounds save the rhythmic breathing of the three persons at the table.

The clairvoyant folded his hands together. "We implore you to go to the light. You are dead and on this earth plane there is nothing more for you. In the kingdom of light others will help you."

Teresa thought that one window shade rippled at the sill, but she couldn't be certain.

As the summer days stretched into weeks and the weeks into months, hundreds of people besieged the homeowners, all wanting tours of the "spook" house. Children told their wide-eyed classmates that caskets floated from room to room and skeletons rattled up and down the staircase. All nonsense, of course.

The Montgomerys finally posted a NO SIGHTSEERS sign on the door, but it had no effect. In one week alone two hundred cars a day disgorged noisy ghost hunters, and on one Sunday seven hundred people broke the front steps trying to gain entry to the house. Teresa, exhausted from the turbulent publicity, refused to admit anyone unless they had written her a letter first. And letters were arriving daily from all parts of Canada.

Charles Montgomery resented the flood of letters and the unruly strangers who banged at the door and peeked in the windows at all hours of the day and night. There could be only one solution. The couple would charge admission to tour their home! Surely anyone wishing to see a house "infested" with ghosts would be willing to pay for the privilege.

But Teresa Montgomery didn't reckon on the trouble she would have getting a trade license to operate a "haunted house."

Chilliwack's acting mayor, Al Holden, said that if the council granted her request then the entire neighbourhood would have to be rezoned from residential to commercial. Alderman Bill Nickel said he felt Mrs. Montgomery only wanted to exploit the free publicity she'd received about her claims that ghosts were in her house.

One day Teresa and a friend discovered that the portrait was fading and also *shrinking* in size. They measured it to confirm their suspicions and wondered how such a feat could be accomplished.

Dr. Geoffrey Riddehough, a lecturer in classics at the University of British Columbia and a member of the Psychical Research Society of England, was invited to study the portrait. He came to no conclusions, other than to remark that there are some things happening in the world for which people have no explanation.

Eventually, Teresa grew sick of the portrait and threatened to get rid of it. She did. The Pacific National Exhibition displayed it for a while, and in 1973 it became the property of a Vancouver radio station. Press accounts do not mention the picture's condition at that time.

Were the accounts of the Chilliwack haunting genuine? That question is impossible to answer. The local journalist who first broke the story said Mrs. Montgomery told her the painting would put the little town on the map. That it certainly did. But the reporter spent many hours and days in the house and, according to an interview with her, ". . . never saw anything or heard anything to suggest the place was haunted."

In 1972 the Montgomerys sold the house and moved to Vancouver Island to enjoy a more tranquil life in a house presumably free of unwanted guests.

The new owner stayed in the mansion for barely a year.

He said that he and his family were moving for personal reasons. He did not elaborate. The house sold for $23,000 to a young Chilliwack couple who intended to renovate it and raise a family there. The new buyers knew the ghost legend, but didn't think much of it.

A Chilliwack real estate agent who handled the sale said the transaction was not that difficult, despite the house's history.

"It used to be that selling a haunted house was a real estate man's nightmare," he told a Canadian Press reporter. "But not anymore. Today, haunted houses seem to attract more interest than those that are not . . ."

If the new owners ever did start seeing strange sights and hearing unusual noises in their notorious home, they had only to call the agent for reassurance that no one else shared their house. You see, the realtor did not believe in ghosts.

NOTE: Certain names in this story have been changed.

AND GHOST MAKES FOUR

Toronto, Ontario

A pleasant avenue in suburban Toronto would seem an unlikely place to find the supernatural, but don't tell that to one young couple who moved into the basement apartment of a neat brick home on just such a boulevard.

The series of events that inexplicably plagued the pair were serious enough to warrant a "dehaunting" by Ian Currie and Carole Davis, two Canadian investigators of the paranormal.

Twenty-year-old Rob, his wife Cindy, nineteen, and their infant son had been in their new apartment barely a month when a growling sound coming from their child's room startled them awake late one night. The couple found the tyke standing up in bed staring at the wall. He seemed scared about something, his mother said. The source of the menacing growl remained a puzzlement.

Over the next few weeks, the child experienced further episodes of sudden crying and screaming. The couple were at a loss to explain his fearful outbursts.

Other freakish occurrences scared Rob and Cindy. A

coffee-maker spurted hot water for no apparent reason, a window slammed shut on a still night, and, most incredible of all, a glass full of milk glided halfway across a table as the couple looked on in amazement. When a friend stayed overnight in the baby's room, she told Cindy about being awakened by a breeze across her face, and of seeing a pallid, yellow light shining down from above.

The couple found out about Ian Currie, an author and former professor, and Carole Davis, a psychic who claimed to have helped police in Canada and the United States. Their little apartment needed, the parents decided, a professional ghost-cleansing.

Currie and Davis claimed to have dehaunted nearly sixty homes at the rate of $250 per house. "Satisfaction guaranteed," Currie told newspaper reporter Gerald Volgenau.

Davis had been in the apartment only a short while when she pronounced it definitely haunted. But the ghost was not an evil presence, "just a poor person in distress," she said. Further, she sensed the presence was that of a dark-haired young man killed in a traffic accident.

Psychic Davis went into a trance with Currie at her side. Within minutes, she was speaking for the ghost — of the driving rain, of the darkness and sudden headlights, of the trouble he had caused for his loved ones, and of his desire to go home. Meanwhile, Ian Currie was talking soothingly to his unseen listener, telling him that he was dead, that the accident was not his fault. He should "go into the light."

Soon the psychic was quiet, her head jerking slightly as if to clear it of the last vestiges of the visiting spirit.

Cindy was stunned at the scene. She had known just such a man, a young acquaintance who had been drinking one night and stumbled in front of an oncoming car during a rainstorm. He was killed instantly.

It can only be surmised that his ghost had for some reason attached itself to the young couple. But now he was gone, Currie and Davis said. Rob and Cindy were relieved. The apartment was definitely *not* big enough for four.

FATHER GHOST

Montreal, Quebec

The Reverend Humphrey Oswald Slattery thought he was quite alone as he knelt at the altar of St. John the Evangelist Episcopal Church saying his evening devotions. Quite unexpectedly, a chair scraped across the worn stone floor from somewhere toward the back of the empty church. Footsteps came up the centre aisle and paused, as if the person were genuflecting. Father Slattery was surprised at the unanticipated intrusion. He turned around to greet the visitor. No one was there.

The ghost of Father Edmund Wood was paying a visit.

During the late 1970s, stories circulated that Father Wood, who died in 1909, was making regular visits to the church he had founded over a hundred years ago. But unlike some encounters with departed souls, those churchmen who believed Father Wood was back did not feel threatened or frightened.

Father Slattery, for instance, said the ghost's presence gave him a feeling of "physical warmth." The damp, stone church would suddenly be filled with "something spiritual," he told reporter Ron Caylor, adding that "many times I have felt despondent, but after encountering Father Wood's presence I leave with a stronger feeling. It's almost like someone's patted you on the back."

Sometimes the priest's ghost would simply play practical jokes, such as hiding objects like devotional candles for several days and then putting them back exactly where they should have been.

Even though Father Wood did not terrorize or disrupt church activities, his occasional wanderings had the capacity to send unwary witnesses into flight. That is what happened to Pastor Harold Parsons. He had been ringing the steeple bells when he had the overwhelming sense that someone else was with him. "I could feel someone behind me get up," he said. At the same time the air seemed to warm significantly. The pastor stopped in midtoll and left the church.

DISTURBING THE DEAD

Vancouver, British Columbia

His name was Johnny.

For a period of time in the 1970s, he was the best friend of a little boy who lived in a Premier Street condominium with his single mother.

Johnny was every lonely boy's dream pal. Tall and rugged looking, he made the child laugh out loud as he talked about all kinds of good stuff for hours on end, even if those chats did take place after midnight, which his mother did not especially appreciate.

Unfortunately, Johnny presented a problem for the little boy's mother. He was a ghost with whom only her son could communicate. And she most certainly did not appreciate his presence.

"It started when [my son] was four months old. I found him one night sitting up in bed roaring with laughter — he was completely exhausted," the woman told reporters at the time. "As he grew older, the number of experiences grew. When he was two, I went into his bedroom one night and found it in chaos. Bedding had been ripped, toys smashed, and the legs of his bed had been torn off. I had heard no noises prior to entering his room."

She disciplined the boy, but regretted it later when she realized a two-year-old could not have caused such damage.

Further compounding her anxiety was the speculation by the Tsleil-Wauthuth Nation that Johnny was one of their ancestors — the condominium in which mother and son lived had allegedly been built on the site of the nation's ancient burial ground. An officer of the Vancouver Psychic Society and a Tsleil-Waututh Nation chief tied the haunting to the burial grounds.

Not until the summer of 1976, when the boy was about three, did his mother seriously ponder the reasons for her son's strange behaviour. That summer was a time of bizarre events: a lampshade spun around, cupboard drawers and doors flew open, a food mixer leaped from a wall, and an ornamental bottle took flight and struck a large sofa.

She started reading about psychic phenomena and even experimented with a Ouija board. Until the night the planchette moved of its own accord. A Catholic priest told her to burn it.

Her doctor thought she was having a nervous breakdown until her friends confirmed her stories.

One neighbour said she watched as the mother emptied dirty water from a vase of flowers. After she returned to the kitchen table where the neighbour was sitting, they both noticed water was mysteriously back in the vase.

The same neighbour had seen a swag lamp swinging, while her daughter reported hearing growling voices in the house, had seen pictures move, and saw the lampshade spinning.

Why didn't the mother act earlier? She told a reporter that it wasn't that easy to face what was happening in her home: ". . . for the past couple of years Jason has woken regularly at midnight and talked to Johnny until 4 A.M. — I've heard a grown man's voice talking to [my son]. I just hide under my bedcovers . . . it's really scary."

She said her son first called the invisible visitor Johnny and provided the description of a tall man with fair hair. The boy said he looked like "Daniel Boone in buckskins."

While the local psychic and members of the Tsleil-Waututh Nation claimed Johnny was from the disturbed burial grounds, others were not so certain.

A Vancouver psychologist who investigated the case said the events might have been caused by psychokinesis, the ability of some individuals to possess enough "mind energy" to move objects, and that "Johnny" was merely the boy's way of explaining the events.

The psychologist noted, for example, that the child described Johnny as tall and blond, the same as his father, who was no longer living with the family. "It could be that the child has anthropomorphized the psychic energy," the doctor said.

The boy's mother said the child "suffered a traumatic experience when his father left home. He's extremely lonely, and every child has an imaginary playmate."

For her part, the mother was much more comfortable thinking the cause of the problem was psychokinesis, and not a ghost aggravated that his grave had been disturbed.

TARLTON MATERNITY HOME

Swift Current, Saskatchewan

Marie Gibbs was a young girl of ten living in Swift Current, Saskatchewan, when her father announced that the family would be moving into a large old place he had found. Housing was scarce in the town during those Depression years, and the reasonable rent made the house doubly attractive.

But Marie's mother was not pleased. She and her husband argued over the plan. "I will not move into *that* house," Marie's mother insisted. She lost the argument, however. It was the only house they could afford, her husband insisted.

"Nothing more was said, but I noticed that Mom would never stay in the house alone at night," Marie remembers. She grew to learn the reason for her mother's fears.

"As time went by I heard strange sounds throughout the house, but more so at night when footsteps . . . ascended the stairs and [then went] down an L-shaped hall which led to the bedroom I shared with my older sister," Marie says.

On one night in particular, Marie's father came bustling into the girls' bedroom.

"Are you all right?" he asked, his brow wrinkled in concern. "I heard someone walking around and then the door of your room opened."

The girls assured their worried father that they were both perfectly safe in their beds.

"I must have been dreaming." He smiled.

He said that "so as not to alarm us, I'm sure," Marie says now. It was clear to her that her mother's concerns were shared to some extent by her father.

The peculiar sounds in the night became almost routine for Marie's family, so much so that the matter was hardly discussed. Only after repeated attempts by Marie and her sister did their mother reveal her continued displeasure at being forced to live in the house.

At one time the house had been the "infamous" Tarlton Maternity Home, a private hospital designed solely for expectant mothers, and ruled over by an owner/matron known for her cold demeanour and unsympathetic ways, especially toward women whose babies had been stillborn.

"Eventually she went insane and died in a mental institution," Marie notes. Soon after that the maternity home was closed and the property put up for rent.

Ironically, Marie's sister had been born in the very same room she now shared with Marie. It had once been the Tarlton's delivery room. "Due to a very difficult pregnancy, Mom spent forty days there, and they were forty days in hell," Marie recalls her mother saying, attributing most of her suffering to the matron's cruelty.

Marie believes the mysterious noises of footsteps and opening doors were caused by the ghosts of the many women who died in childbirth, at last coming back to claim their babies in the old delivery room.

Or perhaps, she avers, it might be the matron herself, continuing on her night rounds, always at eleven o'clock — the time when the footsteps are the most pronounced.

The old house once called the Tarlton Maternity Home still stands in Swift Current. Marie Gibbs said she has been told tenants are never retained for very long.

And she knows why.

PEST HOUSE

Beckley Farm, British Columbia

The shortest history of any haunted house in North America may very well have been that of Beckley Farm, built in the late 1860s or very early 1870s (the records are unclear) between Dallas Road, along Victoria's waterfront, and the shore. Within just a few years it had been demolished, but not before it brought death and misfortune to many who lived there — and the belief among Victorians that its unhappy dead wandered the premises.

George E. Nias erected the house, a horse stable, and other outbuildings that he called Beckley Farm. Nias never lived there. For some reason he moved to Australia, and Beckley Farm was abandoned.

The real story of Beckley Farm begins in 1871, when a smallpox epidemic aboard the ship *Prince Alfred* brought renewed attention to it. The vessel travelled among San Francisco, Victoria, and Nanaimo. During a stop in Victoria, seven passengers were found to have the dreaded disease. A decision was quickly made that the infected people would be sent to Beckley Farm to live in isolation. The house was hurriedly repaired, and a yellow flag was put up to give notice that the farm was now a "pest house."

The *Prince Alfred* continued on its route to Nanaimo, further up Vancouver Island on the Strait of Georgia, and then back down to Victoria. A crewman was diagnosed with smallpox at the second Victoria stop, and he too was sent to Beckley Farm.

One of the original seven passengers, a teenager named Bertha Whitney, died on June 23, 1872. The sailor from the *Prince Alfred* also succumbed to the disease. Both were buried on the grounds of Beckley Farm.

The two deaths were responsible for the first rumours that Beckley Farm was unlucky, even though the six other passengers from the ship fully recovered. Once they got well and left, the farm was again abandoned.

A few months later, a stranger who gave his name as P. Lackle of San Francisco checked into Victoria's old Angel Hotel. He stayed to himself for several weeks, but then revealed to the hotel manager that his wife would soon be arriving from England and they would need some place to live.

The manager suggested he look into the old pest house, Beckley Farm.

That he did. For several days, he was seen wandering around the property, taking notes on what presumably would be the repairs needed to make the house habitable.

Then one morning quite a strange incident was reported. A tenant at the Angel Hotel happened to be walking near Beckley Farm. As he neared the house, he noticed the man known as Lackle and a woman engaged in a heated argument. The woman suddenly struck Lackle and fled. Nobody reported seeing her again.

The man who called himself P. Lackle was found dead

of a self-inflicted bullet wound on February 17, 1873, in a Beckley Farm stable. His last name was actually Stocker and he was from Scotland. No one could find out what his real business in Victoria had been, nor why he had assumed a false identity.

Since the woman who struck him had vanished, the speculation was that he had murdered her and then killed himself. Four deaths were now tied to Beckley Farm. Victorians started reporting weird things at the place — lights glimpsed in some of the old buildings, and a woman's dreadful screams.

The haunting did not last long. The buildings mysteriously burned down in late 1873. A cause was not found, although it was presumed the lights people saw were somehow responsible.

There is a final, tragic footnote to the saga of Beckley Farm.

A woman who had been one of the original passengers quarantined at Beckley Farm, and who survived the ordeal, had settled in New Westminster. Once, as she was sorting through her clothing, she came upon a dress she had owned for many years. She sent it to a dressmaker for alterations. Within days, the dressmaker and several assistants became virulently ill and died. A doctor diagnosed the deaths as smallpox, and speculated that the pox virus had been transmitted in the dress.

Any physical evidence that Beckley Farm ever existed has long since vanished and been forgotten. There is no sentimentality for such a cursed existence.

MUSEUM SPECTRES

Toronto, Ontario

On Queen's Park Crescent, the Royal Ontario Museum may have two old ghosts as part of its impressive collection.

The better known of the pair may be the ghost of the museum's former director, Dr. Charles Currelly, who was eighty-two when he died in 1957. He was director of the museum for thirty-two years, from 1914 until his retirement in 1946.

Dr. Currelly isn't a frightening spectre at all, just peculiarly dressed. He wears a nightshirt and cap as he scurries down the corridor. Precisely why he is dressed this way, or the reason for his haste, is not known.

A little curly-haired blond girl of about eight was seen in the planetarium section of the museum in the late 1970s. She wore a starched white dress and looked very unhappy, according to one museum staff member. Unfortunately, as with many ghosts, no one knew her name or the nature of her distress.

ISLE OF SKYE

Holyrood, Newfoundland and Labrador

This small community of two thousand people on the south end of Conception Bay has an ancient connection to the sea and seafaring ways.

Back in the 1860s, John Mackay and his stepfather, John Cunningham, had a big fishing business in the village, in what is called the North Arm of Holyrood. Mackay's schooner was the seventy-ton *Isle of Skye,* a fore-and-after.

In early October 1865, Mackay, Cunningham, and their crew had a full catch from the Labrador banks and made for home. They were last seen on the night of October 10 crossing Notre Dame Bay, northwest of Fogo. There was a frightful nor'easter early the next day and the *Isle of Skye* was lost.

A curious incident on the night of October 11, however, led some Holyrood residents to think Mackay and Cunningham had weathered the storm. At about ten o'clock that night, people living along the seashore on the South Side, west of Runaway Rock, heard loud cries and shouts of "Hello! Breakers ahead!" coming from across the water. Men jumped into their boats and rowed out into the bay to help what they thought was a ship in distress. Bonfires were lit onshore to guide the stricken craft.

Though the search went on for hours, no sign of a ship was ever found. The shouts had died away; the rescuers went home puzzled. And afraid.

Shortly after retiring for that same night, Denis Penney, who lived along the coast near North Arm, heard the splash and dropping chain of an anchor. His son had been aboard the *Isle of Skye*. Penney was certain the schooner had returned. He got up to light the fire, fully expecting his boy to walk through the door soon.

It didn't happen.

Sometime later, wreckage of the *Isle of Skye* was found at Moulton's Harbour Head, near Twillingate on the northeast coast, several hundred kilometres from Holyrood.

Many believed Mackay and Cunningham attempted to make it home in spirit, if not in the flesh.

THE RAVEN, NEVERMORE

Somewhere off the coast of Haiti

Men and women of the sea know better than to ignore maritime superstitions. No other group may have as many omens, premonitions, or warnings of impending doom as do those who make their living upon the world's oceans.

There are at least two superstitions that should not be disregarded if one is to travel safely across the seas, for to do so is to risk facing the same fate as the *Raven,* a yacht manned by Canadian sailors that was wrecked on a Caribbean reef decades ago.

The ketch was under two oppressive shrouds — its name had been changed, from the original *Danebrog* at its launch to the *Raven,* and, worse still, the name was now that of a bird. Wise sailors avoid those taboos.

But there was more to the *Raven*'s problems than her transgression of seafaring superstitions. The ghost of her original builder prowled the decks.

The ship, then called the *Danebrog*, was under construction in Denmark in 1921 when the builder fell to his death from the dock. It is not clear if there was an investigation, and neither is it certain whether the death was simply an accident.

From 1921 to 1972 — the year the ship was wrecked on a Caribbean reef — the record of the *Danebrog* is unknown. But in the early 1970s, Jan deGroot, head of the Vancouver Sailing Academy, set out to bring the Danish ship to British Columbia from Nassau. He offered Vancouver sailing students the opportunity to serve as crew for $1,000, including airfare to Nassau. They would assist deGroot on the long voyage to British Columbia.

But when the sailing students, deGroot, his wife, and twenty-four-year-old Joan Whiteley arrived in Nassau, the group found a serious problem on board the now-renamed *Raven*.

The American crewmen who had steered the ship from Denmark to the Bahamas said the ship was cursed. Accidents plagued the yacht during its transatlantic voyage, footsteps clattered across the decks when no one should have been there, and, worst of all, the ship had almost sunk in the Bay of Biscay.

Some crew members whispered that they had even seen the ghost of the dead builder. Not one of them volunteered to stay aboard to Vancouver.

So deGroot and his twenty-two-member crew left Nassau under Dutch captain Bert Mooy. The plan was to briefly dock in Haiti and contravene the superstition about the boat's name by changing it back to the *Danebrog*. But since the captain was Dutch, the change had to be made in a Netherlands-governed port. DeGroot decided to leave Haiti for Jamaica and then sail on to the port of Curaçao in the Netherlands Antilles.

Shortly after leaving Port-au-Prince, however, the curse of the *Raven* became visible.

Joan Whiteley was sleeping belowdecks shortly before her 4 A.M. watch began when something awakened her.

"I was in my cabin trying to get some sleep . . . Suddenly I felt a creepy feeling and when I looked up there was a man in blue standing there," she later reported. "He appeared to be ordering a crew about and waving his arms in the air."

The ghost was middle-aged, dressed in clothing of the 1920s. Whiteley thought it was the ghost of the ship's builder.

Four hours later the *Raven* struck a reef near Haiti. Whiteley then had her second brush with the supernatural as she sat in the wheelhouse with deGroot's wife, Elsie.

"We were firmly stuck on the reef and in no danger of sinking. I felt this clammy and creepy feeling again. Tears started to come from my eyes and I felt the ghost leave the ship."

Joan Whiteley believed there was nothing that could have been done to save the ship. The *Raven* was jinxed from the moment the builder was killed. It was just a matter of time . . .

YORKVILLE APPARITIONS

Toronto, Ontario

Whenever old houses are converted to more modern uses, say offices or trendy shops, incorporeal residents of those selfsame dwellings can put a chill into any business climate. Such was the case in two circa-1900 Yorkville homes.

A house on Hazelton Avenue was remodelled into offices for a music production company, but that didn't stop the vocalizings of a female ghost. A company executive working late heard the singing while locking up for the night. He said it was quite a "beautiful" sound. But, so far as is known, no attempt was made to sign her to a contract.

A psychic who worked in the house some years ago said it may have been a woman who lived there during World War II, and was still waiting for her husband to return. The woman was once seen walking down a second-floor hallway, and thence through a wall and front window.

Another man claimed the alarm system, which used motion detectors and infrared light beams, was always going off. The police eventually refused to respond to any alarms at the house, he said.

The people who built a house on nearby Roxborough Street may be still looking after the place — almost a century later. According to reports from 1986, the woman who ran a business there said her cat always acted strangely in the house. A medium was consulted, and she said there were several friendly ghosts present. To a spirit, they were happy with what the woman was doing with their old house, the medium said, and only wanted to protect what had been theirs in life.

A CHANCE ENCOUNTER

Montreal, Quebec

Emile Charles Hamel was a prominent journalist, writer, and former Radio Canada employee in Montreal. So it was not surprising to Pierrette Champoux, herself a celebrated author and television commentator, when she encountered her old friend at the 1961 convention of the Canadian Association of Journalists at the Queen Elizabeth Hotel.

They exchanged pleasantries for several minutes and parted. The only oddity in the encounter was Pierrette's distinct impression that Emile had left something unsaid.

He certainly had. What he didn't tell her was that she had just completed a conversation with a ghost.

Pierrette Champoux has had a distinguished career as a writer, fashion analyst, broadcaster, and world traveller. Indeed, her journeys have taken her to the far corners of the world, allowed her to meet the famous and influential, and given her many fascinating adventures. She has written about her life in newspapers, magazines, and in her most recent books, *Parle-moi du Canada/Talk to me of*

Canada, Raconte-moi Montréal, and *Les Pionnières.* Her unique style even extends to sending personal stationery embossed with her picture standing amidst a smiling group of Uganda pygmies during one of her African safaris.

Nothing in her public life, however, prepared her for the 1961 adventure with a ghost that she later recounted to author Eileen Sonin.

At about mid-afternoon of Saturday, November 18, 1961, Pierrette had left a pleasant gathering of fellow journalists attending the convention. The meetings were going well, lunch had been served, but Pierrette had decided to take her leave.

Just short of the exit, a hand reached out to touch her arm. She turned to see the writer Emile Charles Hamel, a good friend of both Pierrette and her sister. She had not seen Emile for some time. He graciously kissed her hand and they chatted amiably about her recent experiences, and all the work he had to finish. When she asked if it was quite a lot, he nodded in agreement. "A great deal of work that I have at this time," he phrased it.

She declined his invitation to partake of the dwindling buffet she had already lunched on — and Emile and Pierrette warmly shook hands. He said they ought to see more of each other and, she later recalled, it seemed that something else was on his mind. But he didn't say anything more and strode away.

The incident passed from Pierrette's mind. On Monday evening, two days hence, her sister chanced to mention that she had seen a news item in Saturday's newspaper about the sudden death that morning of their friend — Emile Charles Hamel.

Pierrette Champoux was flabbergasted. The newspaper

must be in error, she said, because he had been alive and well Saturday afternoon.

"It isn't as if I merely recognized him across the dining room," she told writer Eileen Sonin. "He stopped me as I was leaving, he kissed my hand, and we chatted together for quite a time. I know it was Emile. I surely recognize my friends when I meet them."

But her sister was just as insistent that it couldn't have been him because the newspaper said he had died at about 8 A.M., a half dozen hours *before* Pierrette said she had talked to him at the Queen Elizabeth Hotel.

Pierrette placed a telephone call to General de Verdun Hospital, where the newspaper said he had died. They confirmed the news. Emile Hamel had been an emergency admittance Friday night and had died quite unexpectedly Saturday morning.

Pierrette could not believe what all the evidence, and her respect for the facts, pointed to — that *somehow* and for some *reason* she had chatted with Emile's ghost. It didn't make sense to this woman used to dealing with the real world and its verifiable details.

For the next week, Pierrette closely examined the many articles written in the Quebec press about Emile's death. He had been a prominent member of the media, and thus his untimely passing attracted wide attention. The photographs of him in the articles were definitely of the man Pierrette saw at the hotel. But that was about all of which she was confident.

"I was so nervous and upset," she said. Even her parish priest assured her that he believed what had happened to her. In fact, he added, he wished the same experience would befall him!

Pierrette Champoux has had several other experiences

with the supernatural since that 1961 meeting with Emile Charles Hamel's ghost. She intends to publish her experiences in a book.

Still, she is perplexed about that first incident. Why did he choose *her* to visit? Why was her conversation with a *ghost* so normal, so completely ordinary? It would seem that more important news would be passed between the corporeal and incorporeal.

The questions have never been answered. However, Pierrette has never disputed the reality of the chance encounter — she spoke with a man who had been dead for several hours and never once thought anything was out of the ordinary. Of that she is entirely and forever certain.

THE HITCHER

Vancouver, British Columbia

Lest one mistakenly believe that the only phantoms in Vancouver reside in old mansions, this spectacular city on the Strait of Georgia has provided refuge for all manner of forms from another world.

The tragic death of a young woman, a student at the University of British Columbia, is the impetus for another Vancouver ghost tale. She has become a hitchhiking ghost, a Canadian version of Chicago's famous Resurrection Mary.

It is said the woman was a passenger in the speeding car of another student when it crashed on University Boulevard, killing her. She lingers there, waiting for a ride to her parents' home. She vanishes when a car stops, one version of the story goes, but in another climbs in and gives her parents' address. When the driver arrives there, she has disappeared.

Ethereal young women waiting alongside highways appear in ghost tales known in virtually every state and province of North America. The Vancouver variant differs only in localizing it to a UBC student.

THE TOMBSTONE

Hamilton, Ontario

Mike Cino's demolition firm had nearly finished ripping apart the second floor of the old building they'd been hired to raze in Hamilton during the fall of 1982. The work was progressing smoothly. Nothing untoward or terribly unusual had happened. The workers had found the customary odds and ends and bric-a-brac in the place, but certainly nothing that would set back their timetable.

On this particular day a worker thought he heard a strange noise from within the building as the machines tore into the structure, but he attributed it to the groans of a well-made house reluctantly giving way to the wrecker's ball.

Then they found the tombstone.

Discovered secreted in a wall of the second floor, the stone bore the chiselled words OUR BABY at the top. Below, two names were still clearly discernible: *Martha Louise, 1888* and *Emma Grace, Nov. 9, 1879.*

No one knew who the little children might have been, or why they died. Nor could Mike Cino guess why the stone was placed where it was found, other than the possibility that it might have been used to prop up the wall.

The discovery, however, was critical for helping to solve an eleven-year-old mystery: the possible cause of frightening visits from a ghost witnessed by two former residents.

Norm Bilotti worked in the composing room of the *Hamilton Spectator* in the early 1970s. He lived in the house with his wife, Sherrie. Their brush with the supernatural came quite unexpectedly, in the middle of the night. Twice.

The first time, Norm jerked awake when his wife screamed at the top of her lungs from the bed next to him. He blinked in the gloomy darkness until he was able to focus on what his wife saw — a human form wearing a long gown hovering above their bed. He couldn't see any face. He had no idea if it was male or female. Only that it was there.

"If she had only seen it herself, I would have thought she was crazy," Norm said in a Canadian Press account of the incident. "If it had only been me, I would have thought I was crazy. But both of us saw it."

The figure vanished when Norm turned on the light.

The second time they knew for *certain* neither was dreaming. Norm saw it first this night, and his cries awoke his wife. A legless woman hovered near them, her eyes protruding grotesquely from her face. And her hair . . . her hair stood on end as if she had stuck her finger in an electrical outlet. She said not a word and then was gone.

Despite the unnerving, middle-of-the-night episodes, the Bilottis had a certain curiosity about the identity of the ghost. They thought a ghost hunter might provide some clues, and called Malcolm Bessent, of Rosary Hill College in Buffalo, New York.

Bessent visited the home and immediately sensed a "presence" in the house. "I think something is concealed in this area — what, I don't know," he said, pointing to a particular section of a wall. "I'm being drawn to it very strongly. It's the reason for the manifestation."

The Bilottis never again were visited by the mysterious woman and moved out of the house shortly thereafter. They thought nothing more would ever be heard about the ghost until . . .

. . . Mike Cino's crew began levelling the old house. He wasn't surprised at finding the nineteenth-century tombstone — after all, he had once found a *bomb* in one place — but it was a bit odd that such a marker would be used to shore up a wall.

Norm Bilotti found out about the discovery. It all made sense, and at the same time chilled the very marrow in his bones.

The tombstone was found *directly above* the bedroom in which the couple had seen the ghost. And further, Malcolm Bessent had pointed to nearly the *precise section of the wall* where the stone was discovered. Norm and Sherrie had seen a ghost . . . and it was somehow connected to the tombstone.

The identity of the two children memorialized on the stone was never established. Was it their mother the Bilottis saw? If so, could this be further evidence that a mother takes care of her children — even after death?

MON PÈRE

Montreal, Quebec

Jocelyne Choquette makes her home on rue Saint-André in the exhilarating cosmopolitan city of Montreal. Until January 11, 1990, she lived at home with her elderly mother and father. On that day, Jocelyne's father, sixty-nine-year-old Phillippe Choquette, passed away.

But that is not quite correct. He passed *on* . . . but he is most definitely not *away*.

To begin with, the moment of Phillippe's death matches nearly exactly that of his sister. She died in July 1987 at the same age, on the same day of the year, and at the same hour as her brother did three years later.

That is only the beginning of this curious story. Phillippe insists upon dropping in unexpectedly on his daughter and wife.

"All through [1993] my father . . . appeared either in dreams or in physical form, giving us advice or warning us of danger," Jocelyne said. "Everything he has said turned out to be true."

Jocelyne's father always appears in the same clothes he had on the day he died.

Not unexpectedly, Jocelyne and her mother didn't receive too much support from the rest of their family when they learned about Phillippe's continued presence.

Jocelyne doesn't mind the skepticism. She is content to have her father very near to her and her mother. She especially likes it when he explains things that later turn out to be true.

"For instance, I had a dream in 1991 about my father. It was two weeks before Christmas. In the dream, my father told me about a big surprise for my mother and me on Christmas Day. He assured us he could do everything and that nothing was refused to him. In anticipation, I was very curious and anxious," she said.

Christmas passed without any "surprise" that Jocelyne or her mother could identify. They didn't know why until a few days later.

"On New Year's Eve, my father appeared very clearly at my side with a look of disappointment. I immediately understood that he was hoping to come back for Christmas as flesh and blood."

Jocelyne's mother, Yvette Lamontagne Choquette, has seen her late husband several times, either in the kitchen or in the living room.

"Very often the sudden smell of his cologne could be detected throughout the room," Jocelyn said. "Sometimes it was followed or preceded by another scent which was very pleasant too."

The appearances of Phillippe happen most often in the morning or in the late afternoon, but rarely at night. Jocelyne's two brothers have never been visited by their late father.

The ghost is also quite insistent in giving advice to his daughter. When she has not followed it, she has had "to go through a lot of problems. Today, when my father gives me advice, I listen to him notwithstanding the fact that it is very difficult to understand everything that is happening to us."

As it would be for anyone.

GHOSTLY BACKUP

Vancouver, British Columbia

In June 1993, employees of Mushroom Studios on West Sixth Street in Vancouver told reporter Peter Clough about a mysterious "back-up" singer whose voice was heard singing "Uh-huh" on an album recorded by folksingers Bourne and MacLeod.

The manager of the studio said the voice may belong to the same ghost who has haunted the building since the late 1970s.

"No one knows for sure who the ghost is, but we discovered that a long, long time ago, this was an Indian ceremonial grounds," the manager said.

She said the spirit is attracted to the music, especially when it includes drums or vocals. Two engineers briefly glimpsed what they thought was the ghost, but could not provide any description.

"THE SPOOKIEST PLACE I KNOW"

Devil's Island, Nova Scotia

With those words Jack Conrod, a longtime caretaker on Devil's Island, a twenty-five-acre chunk of sand and bushes near the harbour entrance to Halifax, Nova Scotia, described the place he knew well. Although it's only a kilometre from Eastern Passage, Conrod said, "it might as well be in the middle of the Atlantic. You can get stranded . . ."

But it's not getting stranded that's worried people, it's wondering if all the hair-raising tales about the island are even remotely true.

Although it was settled in the early eighteenth century, the small, windswept island gained its reputation only in the past century. The reasons are probably twofold: when the sun rose and set, it shone through the lighthouse windows so that it seemed the building was on fire; and many people have died in the rough waters of the reef-rimmed island. Families only occasionally lived there, making a living from fishing, but most of them left decades ago.

In 1977, a man from Whitehorse, Yukon, took up an offer by the island's owner, Bill Mont, to live there rent-free.

He is said to have lasted one week before taking off for parts unknown.

Clarence Henneberry spent the first sixty years of his life on Devil's Island, until he and other residents were forced to leave in 1945 because of wartime military restrictions. Government officials thought they could see too much of the naval activity in and around Halifax Harbour.

Henneberry did not believe in ghosts, but he had enough strange experiences on the island not to fool around with the supernatural.

Across the island from where he grew up there was a house that was thought to harbour evil spirits.

"There was something wrong with the house," Henneberry said. "I've seen the roof of that house ablaze a half dozen times. Once I went up to it and put my hand on it. It was as cold as that kitchen table."

Then there was the "walking light."

The unheld lantern "used to go from the house to the bush, then walked back . . . I wanted to go see it but my father wouldn't let me. I wasn't scared," Henneberry insisted.

In Nova Scotia, as in many other regions of the world, there has been a belief in "forerunners," sometimes called "tokens." These are appearances by dead relatives, or omens of a tragedy to come.

Clarence Henneberry witnessed a forerunner. His brother Charlie appeared to him late one night.

"I woke and he was in my room with wet clothes on. I asked him what he was doing home and he didn't answer me. He was there only a minute."

Henneberry didn't think any more about the incident until the next day. His family received word that Charlie had drowned the night he appeared to Clarence.

THE WOMAN IN CHAINS

Victoria, British Columbia

The Tod House on Heron Street in Oak Bay, the oldest
house in Victoria, could justifiably have been called that
city's most haunted dwelling.

Built in 1848 by Scotsman John Tod, the chief trader
for the Hudson's Bay Company for over forty years, the
sprawling white mansion was originally located on a four-
hundred-acre tract of land. The enormously wealthy and
influential Tod was a member of the first legislative council of Vancouver and, some have written, one of Victoria's
first idle rich.

At his death in 1882 at the age of ninety-one, the tall,
gaunt Tod was the oldest living resident of British
Columbia. One of his pallbearers was the notorious
"hanging judge," Matthew Bailey Begbie.

The Tod House is a wooden structure with giant tim-
bers as its foundation. An owner some years ago, Waveney
Massie, and her husband took great pride in restoring the
house to its earlier glory. They filled the house with early
Canadian antiques and period furnishings. One observer

said the Massies were so effective in their restoration that one could easily believe "John Tod is still master of this house, and can be expected momentarily." The table was always set, as though the Massies were expecting Tod and his dinner guests.

The haunting of Tod House is attributed to Tod's last wife — he married seven times and fathered ten children — a Native woman who may have gone crazy and been kept in chains in a small room.

Two guests in the house many years ago were awakened in the night by the moaning of a female spectre, her wrists and ankles fettered. "They say she was reaching out, as if to implore them to remove her chains," Waveney Massie told a reporter.

Mrs. Massie was always willing to detail the history of the house and its ghostly legacy. She even had her own odd experiences to add.

"This door leading down to the basement and the secret tunnel . . . used to swing open all by itself. And in the sitting room — the rocking chair — it just rocked and rocked. And this old cookie jar, hanging on a hook by the fire, it rocked, too. And one Christmas, the tenants found all their Christmas decorations lying in the middle of the living room floor, and no one knew how they got there," she said.

The entrance to the old tunnel to which Mrs. Massie referred was boarded up, but it supposedly led to a beach below the house.

Mrs. Massie said the Tod House ghost became more restrained after a disquieting incident in the garden. "One of the earlier owners of the house was digging in the garden to install a new oil tank, when he dug up human bones, which crumbled to the touch. No one knows to whom they belonged, but from that time there were no more ghostly experiences."

The experiences of two *Vancouver Sun* reporters who spent a night in the Tod House back in 1950, years before the Massies bought it, lend credence to the Massies' story.

Reporter Chris Crombie and photographer George Vipond didn't actually *see* any ghosts, but there were plenty of other incidents the men were "at a loss to explain."

Crombie wrote:

"In the night we heard the squeak of the white picket fence gate outside as it turned on its hinges, followed by the crunch of footsteps on the path; but nobody came to the door and when we looked there was only the black path and the white fence, brilliant in the moonlight."

The reporter noted that it was three years earlier when the events to which Mrs. Massie referred had taken place. Not only had the owners seen the cookie jar swinging about, but hats were thrown from a rack, a door opened by itself, and "indistinct" voices and footsteps were heard.

At the time Crombie and Vipond visited, the Tod House was owned by Col. T.C. Evans, who had bought it in 1944. The journalists came away "half skeptical, half convinced."

"Shortly after midnight we sat huddled in the guest room where no visitor has ever spent a complete night in slumber and where few have been willing to return for a second night," Crombie wrote. "We heard four muffled but distinct thumps and thought of John Tod's last wife who went insane and was chained in a small lean-to, which is now gone, but once opened into the guest room. We thought of the crazed woman's vain attempts to escape by throwing her body against the walls of her small, stifling prison.

"The light, soft tread of bare feet sent us into the long, high ceilinged hall, but there was nothing, only a splotch of moonlight on the grey-carpeted floor."

And the remembrance of things past.

THE EVIL BED

Scarborough, Ontario

The idea that a piece of furniture can harbour ill will for the living seems a preposterous idea. Surely nails and glue and wood cannot combine to create an entity capable of producing emotional responses, or cause afflictions for its owner.

Yet there is the story of the young mother of two teenage daughters from Scarborough, Ontario, who endured a nightmare of bad luck — because of an old bed. She said it was cursed, and the curse touched all who came in contact with it.

She told her story to reporter Tony Carr:

The woman, whom we shall call Sarah, ran a successful business in the Toronto suburbs in the late 1970s, lived with her two daughters in a nice apartment complex, and, in general, had no reason to doubt that her life would continue on a steady course.

Until the night she found the bed.

"Walking from my car to the elevator, something made me glance at the far corner of the underground parking lot. That's when I first saw the bed. It was beautiful and appeared to have been abandoned," she recalled.

She hauled it up to her apartment, put it together and wondered why anyone would throw away such a splendid piece of furniture.

"I was studying the bed when this weird, very chilling sensation came over me. Blaming it on fatigue, I got ready for my bath and decided the next morning I would buy a mattress and make this lovely old bed my own."

On the night the new mattress was delivered, Sarah was asleep in the bed, which she shared with one of her daughters.

"Something caused me to sit bolt upright," she said. "There at the foot of the bed stood my best girlfriend. Her lips were moving but there was no sound." Sarah's friend lived two floors above her in the same building.

"I remember glancing at the clock. It was 2:03 A.M., and I said, 'Marian, what on earth are you doing here at this hour?'"

Her friend didn't answer, but Sarah's question awoke her daughter.

"Who are you talking to, Mom?" the girl asked. "Mom! What's that blue light by the end of the bed?"

Marian's apparition, appearing only as a blue light to the girl, faded.

Mother and daughter were too upset to go back to sleep. As they sat at the kitchen table, someone knocked at the door. Sarah cautiously opened it a crack.

Two police officers stood at the threshold. After confirming her identity, one of the men asked:

"Do you know a Marian Ducot?"

"Yes, I do," Sarah replied.

"Well, I'm sorry to have to tell you this," one of the officers said, "but she's just been murdered."

The story they told was that Marian had been walking to the elevator in the parking garage when she was jumped by a man wielding a heavy wrench. She was beaten to death. Her killer lived in the apartment directly above Sarah . . . and just below Marian Ducot. The killing had taken place in the parking garage below Sarah's apartment and in almost the same place where she had found the abandoned bed.

The killer could offer no rational explanation for his actions. "I don't know what came over me, it's as though I was possessed," he said later.

Sarah claimed that after the murder of her friend, the bed seemed to become a living thing. She felt the bed "trembling" as she tried to go to sleep later on the night of the killing.

"There was something strange about that bed. Who had thrown it out in the first place? And why? Although I hadn't mentioned the trembling in the bed to my daughters, neither of them would sleep in it. My youngest, who wanted to sleep in it, ran from the room screaming: 'Someone's laughing at me from under the bed.'"

Even more bad fortune descended on the young woman. Her business failed, she said, because of a fire and "unscrupulous wholesalers"; her car was demolished in an accident after the brakes failed "for no apparent reason."

It was the bed, she reasoned. Her problems started when she hauled the bed up to her apartment. Perhaps if she got rid of it, her troubles would cease.

"I tried to sell, but as soon as people saw it, they became frightened. I tried giving it away . . . A junk dealer took it. The next morning my bed was lying against the side of the apartment building."

Finally a friend offered to take it off her hands. He thought the trouble was with Sarah and not with the bed.

But as they reconstructed the bed in his home, Sarah was so overcome with anger she started pounding the bed with a hammer. She really blamed it for her troubles. Her friend chuckled and asked if she thought the bed might start weeping if she hurt it enough. She stopped and agreed that what she was doing seemed pretty silly.

"We were still laughing when I glanced at the bed, and saw something that stopped me cold. Trickling from the hammer marks were little streams of water, as though the bed was crying!"

Her friend attributed the water to condensation dripping from some overhead water pipes. Sarah said they weren't close enough to have that kind of effect.

Unfortunately the bed continued its menacing ways. Seven days later, Sarah had the bed back. It seems her friend's marina business had suddenly folded after a series of freak accidents. He said all the problems had begun the day the bed came into his possession.

There was more, her friend said:

"I wasn't in it [the bed] for an hour when it started vibrating . . . trembling — or something. I didn't believe I'd ever hear myself say this, but the thing seemed to be laughing at me!"

Sarah went to a Toronto psychic who claimed a man had died in agony in the bed after being poisoned and then urged her to burn it if necessary. After the visit, Sarah's fortune seemed to change.

An antiques buff who specialized in fine, old furniture had heard about the bed and offered to buy it. "It's gorgeous," he said after viewing it. "I must have it."

Sarah was honest in telling him about her painful history with the bed, but he would not be dissuaded. He offered her cash and took it the same day.

"My nightmare had ended. I felt as though a great burden had been lifted from my shoulders," she recalled.

The man who bought Sarah's bed added an ironic footnote to the story. It seemed that since he bought the bed, nothing but *good* luck had come his way. His business more than doubled and he gave up the idea of closing it down, which he had been contemplating before he bought the bed. "It's right out of the blue," he said of his successes.

He hadn't slept in it, he said. "But I will, sure. Bad luck won't happen to me."

Sarah hoped her life would return to normal. But she wasn't entirely certain. "Maybe, just maybe, my life and that terrible bed will be intertwined once again . . ."

THE COTTAGE

Saskatchewan Beach, Saskatchewan

During the late 1900s Jean Moore took her two children — then ages seven and four — to a cottage on Saskatchewan Beach for the summer. She was very happy to find such an idyllic warm-weather retreat, but a series of events that took place there one night were so "strange" that Jean still clearly remembers them.

The well-kept cabin had been in the same family for nearly sixty years. It was "marvellous," Jean recalled, noting that a rocking chair, a unique freestanding hammock, and several interesting pieces of wicker furniture remained in the living room. A china cabinet held an eccentric collection of teacups and saucers which Jean and her children used for "elegant" tea parties. "Some of the saucers even matched the cups!" she said.

A narrow staircase led to an attic room that the children called "the tower," in which they would play for hours on rainy summer afternoons.

"We have a good view of the lake from the living room windows," Jean said. "Many times that summer the three of us watched as a storm swept down the lake like a fury draped in grey mist, finally crashing in on us with howling winds and curtains of water."

The children were especially pleased if the electricity went out. Then they were permitted to light the kerosene lamp with its beautiful china bowl and delicately fluted chimney.

On the night Jean Moore remembers so well, the children had been in bed only a short while when a storm rose over the lake. As it bore down on the snug little cottage by the shore, Jean secured the windows and doors more carefully than usual and then went to bed. Her bedroom opened off one side of the living room; her children's rooms were located directly across the living room from her.

"I lay awake in bed for some time, quite happily watching the living room light up with each flash of lightning, and when the thunder finally subsided I drifted off to sleep," Jean said.

"I don't know how long I slept, but the storm was over, and when I woke it was sudden, as though I'd been called from a deep and dreamless state. For a few seconds I was aware only of total silence, total darkness, and of a total, all encompassing, senseless . . . fear. My heart was pounding violently. I was drenched in sweat."

The fear that paralyzed Jean Moore was caused by a sense that there was *something* in the darkness at the foot of her bed. Something in the blackness she could not see. Her eyes seemed to be on stems that reached out and through the night to identify whatever it was that lurked there.

"I couldn't speak or cry out," she said. It was not an intruder, Jean knew. "It wasn't that type of fear."

For what seemed like an eternity, the young mother was immobilized by this silent horror, unable to utter as much as a single syllable.

"Just when I thought my heart would burst, I had the sense that whatever it was, was moving out of my room. It seemed to be shuffling slowly across the living room toward the children's rooms."

Still she was unable to move, even though the thing was heading toward her sleeping tots.

"Mother, is that you?" Jean's seven-year-old son suddenly cried out from his room.

Minutes passed — or was it merely several seconds? — before Jean found her voice.

"Are . . . you . . . all right, son?" Jean's voice was strained as she called back.

"Yes, I'm okay, Mom," came his weak reply.

The sun was shining through the curtained windows when Jean awoke from her fitful sleep. Had she been dreaming? she wondered. A horrible nightmare kindled by the thunderstorm . . . She leaped from bed and ran barefoot across the living room. She threw open the doors to her children's separate rooms. Both were sleeping soundly. A quick check of the windows and outside doors showed they had not been disturbed. Surely there *had* been something about in the cabin last night . . . and yet . . .

At breakfast a few hours later, Jean casually asked her son why he had called out to her during the night.

He paused a few seconds before saying, "Something was in my room."

"What was it?" Jean coaxed.

"I don't know," the boy said thoughtfully, "but it was black and round. I was too scared to turn on the light so

I turned over and pretended to be asleep."

The boy then added a peculiar afterthought. "I think it was smiling at me, though."

He told his mom that when he turned back over to look at where the thing had been, there was nothing there.

Jean Moore still wishes she knew what had been in her cottage.

SLEDDING SIMON

Montreal, Quebec

The most persistent ghost legend in Montreal dates to the eighteenth century and concerns one of the city's most colourful characters: the Scottish fur trading baron Simon McTavish. His ghost is said to rest uneasily in a mausoleum on Mount Royal.

To understand McTavish's continued longing for an earthly existence, it is necessary to know a little about his eccentric personality and extravagant lifestyle, which earned him the nickname of "Le Marquis."

McTavish landed in Canada after living for a number of years in New England during the late 1700s, and established himself in the fur trade. In his early years, he travelled by canoe as far as the Great Lakes buying pelts. He later became a principal owner, with Simon Fraser as one of his partners, of the North-West Company which, from 1780 to 1821, dominated the fur trade throughout most of the North American continent.

The business acumen McTavish exhibited is not what kept most Montrealers enthralled. The man's appetite for

hard work was matched equally by his appetite for food —
and for love! A bachelor most of his life, he said he was
never happy unless he was *in* love, or *falling* in love.
Apparently that happened quite frequently. He was equally famous for his grand parties, and for his craving for
oysters and alcohol, both of which he consumed in prodi-
gious quantities.

McTavish eventually married a beautiful French-
Canadian woman, but it would not be a long union. Therein
lies the beginning of the tale of Simon McTavish's ghost.

The old Scotsman promised his bride that he would
build her the most fabulous mansion in all of Montreal,
atop Mount Royal. But McTavish did not live to enjoy
either his marriage or his new home. He died in 1805 during the construction of the mansion and was buried in a
mausoleum, which can still be seen inside the park that
tops Mount Royal, past the end of rue McTavish. The
mansion was never completed.

The joie de vivre that made the rich fur trader one of
Montreal's great men-about-town might be the reason
legends persist that he continues to roam his old neighbourhood.

His unfinished mansion came to be called the "haunted house of Mount Royal." Some said that for a long time
after McTavish's death, the revelries of great parties
could be heard from within its partly completed walls.
Those with more fanciful imaginations swore that
"fairies" danced on its tin roof. One or two of his old
acquaintances whispered that he died after seeing the
ghost of a former mistress in the mansion during one of
his frequent forays to oversee its construction.

But it is outside, on the wintry slopes of Mount Royal,
that Simon McTavish's ghost is in its element. The scene

can be grim and quite startling: McTavish is sitting up in his coffin, the lid flung open, tobogganing pell-mell down the mountain!

There may be some truth in the reports that *something* ghoulish did at one time come sliding down Mount Royal. An anatomy professor is said to have lived near the abandoned McTavish mansion during the 1870s. He had a hard time acquiring corpses for class demonstrations and thus employed grave robbers to make forays into the newly built Mount Royal and Côte-des-Neiges cemeteries. They may have transported their "acquisitions" down the mountain aboard sleds and into the professor's waiting wagon. Witnesses could be correct in their assertions that a coffin occasionally came coasting down the snowy slopes, but it might not have been Simon McTavish along for the ride.

Then again, who is to say that his ghost might not have liked to have joined the disturbers of the dead for an impromptu, albeit gruesome, toboggan party?

THE HAUNTED GALLERY

Burnaby, British Columbia

Halloween, 1986. Several employees of the Burnaby Art Gallery, housed in an old mansion known as Fairacres, decide to investigate the unused, abandoned third floor of the building. They find dust covering the floor and cobwebs in dark corners. Poking around, the group finds boxes of decades-old debris, an ancient wringer washer. A sink roosts incongruously in the middle of the floor.

They didn't uncover what they were really looking for — some evidence of ghosts. Nor were there signs of recent human habitation. The strangest discovery was the life-size face of a woman, apparently clipped from a magazine and taped to a window. The eyes had been cut out, as if it had once been used as a mask.

The desolation encountered on the third floor was all the more disconcerting because at least one member of the small band had once heard strange noises coming from there, noises that made her think someone lived up there.

"I would hear 'them' opening the window and closing the window," the young woman told a reporter. "And I would hear them walking and banging things."

The experience was so "real," the woman said, that when coworkers told her the third floor had been abandoned years before, she was very surprised.

Had the young art gallery worker known something of the history of Fairacres, she would have understood that eerie sounds ought to be the least of her concerns. For years, various employees have told stories of wispy figures floating down hallways, footsteps in abandoned rooms, and odd sensations of being watched by unseen eyes.

Vancouver businessman Henry Ceperley and his second wife Gracie built Fairacres as their retirement home in 1909. Situated on a rise with a commanding view of Deer Lake Park, the mansion is known for its unique architectural design, stained glass windows which allow sunlight to cast dazzling rainbows on the oaken staircase, and black enamel columns.

Gracie Ceperley died ten years after the home was completed. For possible legal reasons, the house and grounds were in her name. Her will required that the property remain with Henry until he died or sold it. Any money realized from a sale was earmarked for a children's playground at Stanley Park.

For reasons unknown, Henry Ceperley disregarded his wife's will. First Henry Buscombe leased, then purchased the three-storey Edwardian-style mansion from Ceperley. After Buscombe sold the house, and over the ensuing thirty-five years, Fairacres was an extension to Vancouver General Hospital, a private home, and then, from 1939 to 1954, a monastery for the Order of St. Benedict; the monks left when the new Westminster Abbey in Mission was finished.

Fairacres next entered its darkest period, one that some believe may be responsible, in part, for the supernatural events reported there.

For several years in the late 1950s and early 1960s, a charlatan who called himself Archbishop John I, leader of the Society of the Foundation for a More Abundant Life, held sway over untold numbers of Vancouverites. In reality, the so-called archbishop was one William Frank Wolsey, known to law enforcement authorities in the United States and Canada as a convicted bigamist who was also wanted on charges ranging from embezzlement and strongarm collection tactics to wife beating.

Born in Estevan, Saskatchewan, in 1904, Wolsey was a compelling personality with piercing blue-grey eyes above an iron-grey beard. He bought Fairacres and turned it into his church and school.

The lessons he taught were dreadful.

Children were told they would die unless they believed what was taught to them. One boy with a communications disorder was mocked during a sermon and became so traumatized that he reverted to baby talk. A young mother kept her infant son in a darkened closet for several months on instructions from Wolsey. The regular curriculum was called "bio-psychology"; Wolsey personally taught a class in sex and hygiene.

The *Vancouver Sun* published an exposé of Wolsey in 1959 and his purported miracles, but his "religious" empire didn't collapse until the mid-1960s, when members started leaving and the courts froze the church's assets of $2 million. Wolsey fled Canada and disappeared.

The Burnaby council purchased the property in 1966 as a centennial project and converted it into an art gallery, which it remains to this day.

A wife whose final wishes were ignored by her husband and a fraudulent religious sect whose traumatized members may never have recovered from their experiences: either event may of itself be enough for all manner of paranormal activity, but taken together there seems to be evidence that Fairacres' history provides some explanation for the experiences various persons have said they had there over the years.

A former gallery director told a reporter about the ghost of a woman in a dark blue gown:

"People have seen and heard a presence in the building. A woman in an evening dress . . . She was seen once upstairs and once downstairs. People are uncomfortable in the building. No one likes to stay late by themselves. [But] there's been no murders or no deaths that we know of — no real stories to explain it."

The problem of staff not wanting to work after hours was so serious that this former director included a lengthy reference to it in his final report to the gallery board, five months after his resignation.

"Staff members have firsthand experience of the presence of 'spirits' and usually decline to work in the evening (even early evening) alone," he wrote. "While this situation may be taken lightly by the Board, it IS a matter of concern when staff are not willing to work in the evening."

But a gallery director in the late 1980s said that he'd had no experience at all with ghosts at Fairacres, even on those late evenings when he was responsible for locking up.

Several news articles from the mid-1960s discuss the appearance to some staff members of the "wispy shape" of a woman. A caretaker said he saw a woman in "a long, transparent, flowing gown" walking down the corridor of the abandoned third floor. That's where "Archbishop John I" housed the children of his followers.

A gallery worker in the mid-1980s found that whatever might haunt Burnaby Gallery is something of a prankster. Working over a basement workbench, he had been removing prints from their frames using a hammer and screwdriver. He was distracted for a moment, and when he turned back his tools had been placed neatly on a wall rack — two metres away from where he'd been working!

Later, he took some empty picture frames to an old wine cellar used for storage. As he approached, the padlock on the cellar door was swaying back and forth, though he hadn't touched it. He watched the movement for some time before it stopped.

Another employee learned that not only have people seen the ghost of a woman on the uppermost floor, but that she may also traipse down the stairs to the second floor. He was preparing walls on the main floor for an upcoming exhibit and a colleague was working in the basement (the same man whose tools moved of their own accord). He told a reporter what happened next.

"I heard someone walk from the outside deck [at one time a bedroom balcony] from one corner of the second floor across to the other diagonally. This is a very old building and when someone walks across the deck it sounds throughout the building. The floors weren't carpeted then — it wasn't shoes, you could hear the pressure on the wood like slippers or stocking feet."

He called his friend up from the basement and together they scoured the building.

"There's no way they could have got past us, not with two people. If they'd went out the french doors, the alarm would have gone off. There were no open windows, and even if there were, it's a long two-storey drop, twenty-five feet or more."

Sometimes the sense of a presence is so strong that one has to leave a room or a building to keep one's balance. This was the case with a gallery officer in 1984. She was at the front desk waiting for several others to arrive for an evening meeting when she heard the rustle of satin or taffeta coming from behind her.

"I was very intent on preparing my notes and I heard this noise," she said. "I wasn't frightened, I looked over and there was nothing there. About four minutes later the sound grew louder. My intuition warned me that something was trying to communicate. I knew there was something there that was not of this world . . . I certainly didn't want to see it."

She walked outside and waited in her car until her colleagues arrived for the meeting. That's where they found her, in the parking lot with her car doors locked.

If there are entities at Fairacres trying to communicate with the living, psychic Joan Fontaine identified at least a few of them for a CBC special in 1987.

She found two areas of the mansion to be especially heavily "populated" — both locations are in the basement, including the wine cellar with the oscillating lock.

Fontaine also heard children crying. "This is a very

unhappy place," she concluded.

In an upstairs room once used as a maid's bedroom, Fontaine felt someone invisible brush past her, a man who gave his name as Joseph.

In the television program, Fontaine said an exorcism wouldn't work. Fairacres would simply attract more ghosts.

The current management of Burnaby Art Gallery will not discuss the ghostly legacy of Fairacres.

UNCONSECRATED GROUND

Holyrood, Newfoundland and Labrador

Jim Curran's ghost proved the adage that one had better follow a dying man's wishes, or face the consequences.

Curran told his son-in-law, James Butler, that he wanted to be buried in the new cemetery on Holyrood's South Side, even though it wasn't technically "open" as of yet.

"If you don't," Curran said, "I will return and give you not a moment's peace."

Curran died just before Christmas. Butler passed along his father-in-law's request for burial in the new cemetery to Father Walsh.

"Impossible," the pastor pronounced. "I won't hear of such a thing. The cemetery is not consecrated. We'll bury Mr. Curran on the North Side and if he's set to come and haunt anyone, let it be me."

Butler said that would be fine, as long as the ghost didn't come to visit him.

Jim Curran was laid to rest on a snowy afternoon shortly after Christmas. Father Walsh and his driver made for home, which was at Harbour Main. The snowstorm got worse and the men found the road blocked. They took a path across a pond but wandered for three hours before they found their way back. Father Walsh's driver, a superstitious fellow named Harry, was badly rattled.

"It's Jim Curran's ghost what led us wrong," he swore.

Father Walsh heard grumblings among his congregation that maybe the old man should have been buried in the new cemetery. In church the next Sunday, the priest explained his reasons for not allowing anyone to be buried in the South Side graveyard until it was blessed. He would take more convincing, it seemed.

Later that night, Walsh heard a knock at his front door. He opened it to find no one there, but did hear distinct footsteps cross the threshold, walk across the floor and thence up the staircase to a bedroom.

Another priest in the region, Father O'Donnell, came to visit the next day. He inquired about the visitor Father Walsh had received the previous night. Walsh denied anyone had been there, but Father O'Donnell said he knew better.

That was enough for Father Walsh. He ordered the cemetery opened immediately. The first order of business was the exhumation of Jim Curran's body from his North Side grave and reburial in the new cemetery.

The old man who was disobeyed has rested serenely ever since.

BALDOONIGANS

Baldoon, Ontario

Old John McDonald had a farm. A haunted farm, and a most famous one in Canadian ghostlore. The sleepy hamlet of Baldoon, in southern Ontario, rarely saw activity of any sort in 1829. But when farmer McDonald came into town to report what was happening at his place, the rest of frontier Canada soon took notice. McDonald said supernatural forces had nearly succeeded in destroying his family. What he had was the work of a poltergeist.

Large chunks of timber were flying around his barn. Soon, pots and pans and other household objects were being hurled through the air without any sign of human assistance.

Small projectiles — which Mrs. McDonald called "witch balls" — pounded against the outside walls.

The poltergeist fired objects inside and outside the house on an almost daily basis. The intensity of the peltings varied, but rarely let up entirely. Sightseers flocked to the farm to see for themselves the strange phenomena.

A few said they heard "strange moans" that seemed to come from everywhere, yet nowhere.

For a long three years the poltergeist kept up its antics. The McDonalds grew increasingly despondent. They tried all sorts of methods to rid their farm of the haunting — even calling in a "witch hunter" — but to no avail.

The phenomena stopped without explanation in 1831. Nothing more was seen, felt, or heard of the Baldoon poltergeist. The McDonalds resumed their quiet, rural life. It remains one of Canada's enduring supernatural mysteries.

CLOSE ENCOUNTERS

Vancouver, British Columbia

It sounded like a voice. A wail. Someone in deepest agony. Yet it wasn't quite human. Not like any human they'd ever heard. The family thought it might be their little dog, whining in a most singular way. That is until the night when they heard the yowl and at the same time saw the dog cowering at the foot of a bed.

Then they knew something else was in their house. And they didn't want any part of it.

The nine children lived with their fisherman father in a house they'd occupied for twenty-four years. The mother had recently passed away. It was summer 1978.

An official of a Vancouver psychic society, Linda Klor, learned about the story. She said the family first heard the alarming noise in the middle of the night, but it seemed "more like a voice than a noise."

On the second occasion, the family mistakenly thought their dog was the source of the problem. They also heard the "voice" utter a word that sounded like "die" or "why."

When it happened on a third night, father and children

decided to spend the next night elsewhere. A tape recorder was left on, however, to pick up any sounds in the ostensibly empty house. Their dog also remained behind.

Linda Klor told reporters that the recorder taped the dog's barks — but also what "sounded like someone in deep agony. And whatever the entity was, it was using the energy of that dog's bark."

The distressed voice on the tape was not the only noise recorded. Heavy footsteps pounded across the floor, rattling glasses on a nearby table.

Klor and another medium visited the house. They sensed a man present, "a very confused entity," but one whom they could not otherwise identify.

The house seemed to quiet down after that. There was a final wailing sound, but then silence. Klor reported that an electronic analysis of the tape found the voice was not human. She said there did not seem to be an explanation for the events.

CHILDREN OF THE NIGHT

Montreal, Quebec

Sometimes it is better not to question Providence. Yet the intervention of coincidence or chance or God or whatever one chooses to call it is not always heeded by prudent men and women.

Such was the case in nineteenth-century Montreal at a municipal facility that housed incorrigible children. Built in 1805 in the design of a secure but "homey" structure, the place was soon struck with tragedy. Two children killed the director and his wife and set the house ablaze to cover up their crime. They were soon apprehended and put on trial for murder. They were quickly found guilty of the slayings — and hanged.

That should have been the end of this particular brutality, but it wasn't. The house was rebuilt on its original foundation and passed from owner to owner for the next hundred years. If it is possible for a *locale* to be haunted by past events, this is one of those cases. Murder, suicide, and more unexplained fires plagued the numerous habitués of this cursed house. Zones of frigid air suddenly sprang up in the warmest of its rooms.

In 1905, author Paul Fortier, his pretty young wife Denise, and their lively five-year-old daughter Gisele bought the home and moved in. They knew little of its history. They should have been more careful.

Fortier's inaugural novel, *Fields of Amaranth,* had just been published to generally positive reviews. He had nearly completed a second book and was looking forward to spending his writing career in the distinctive old house.

Denise Fortier was the first to discover the true legacy of the home. Its role in a heinous crime early in the last century was well known in the neighbourhood, and perhaps to the real estate agents as well, but everyone failed to warn the Fortiers. Perhaps this was an accident, perhaps it was something more. At any rate, when Denise spoke to neighbours about their home, the story of its past settled heavily on her conscience.

She grew more apprehensive with each passing week. Then her little daughter, Gisele, became affected. The child barely slept through the night; her bedroom seemed afflicted with gnawing cold spots. Perhaps, too, she sensed her mother's increasingly anxious moods. The poor tot could do little but worry that *"ma mère"* was upset about . . . something.

Denise's visit with her parish priest did little to absolve her of the gnawing fear; he thought the strain of keeping up the large house was too much for her. When she asked him to exorcise her home, he sent her away with more than a little skepticism in his dismissive tone.

Denise came home from the church with the almost palpable understanding that on this night there would come something truly horrible.

Paul seemed especially churlish at dinner. He consumed

75

nearly a full bottle of wine and spoke little to either his wife or his daughter. His behaviour had changed since moving into the house, and he snapped at Denise whenever she tried to broach the subject of his erratic comportment. He just laughed when she tried to point out those rooms in the house that seemed unnaturally cold, or those in which there seemed to be several pairs of eyes watching her every move. She hardly dared mention those other times when she heard childish laughter that sent chills as cold as the grave itself through her entire body.

The evening was a disaster. Denise knew better than to let Gisele linger too long in such an atmosphere. She carried the child up to bed, whispering all the while that the bright morning sun would cheer them all.

Gisele shook her head. She held her mother tight, begging her to take her away from the house that night. A cold spot had been in her bed last night, she cried. She was afraid it would come back.

Denise tucked the child in and kissed her goodnight Gisele held on to her mother with all the might she could muster in her tiny arms. It was as if to let her mother go would mean the end of her small family.

The events of the next few hours were eventually pieced together from Gisele's tortured memories and the testimony of a few witnesses.

Some hours after she fell asleep, Gisele awoke to the smell of smoke. There were no flames visible nor any sense of extreme heat. She ran down the hallway. Smoke was coming from beneath her parents' bedroom door. She pushed the door open. The bedroom was an inferno. But there was a more horrible sight — her father's lifeless body sprawled on the floor, a pair of scissors buried in his throat; only the bloodied handles were visible. Gisele's eyes shifted to the bed where her frenzied mother was fighting off two small, naked boys who were shaking with soundless laughter as they drove their fists into Denise's bruised and bloody face.

Gisele ran next door for help. When the neighbours arrived the scene was not at all as she had breathlessly related to them. Yes, Paul Fortier's remains were on the floor and Denise was barely conscious on the bed — but there was no fire, no frenzied, naked boys, no smell of smoke. Only the indisputable signs of a murderous quarrel between husband and wife. Denise had apparently fought off her husband's attack by stabbing him in self-defence with the scissors.

That was the verdict of the police, anyway. They dismissed Gisele's account as the sad result of having seen her mother kill her father. Denise lived for several months before succumbing to her critical injuries. She never regained consciousness.

Gisele Fortier moved away to the United States to live with her grandparents.

The Fortiers were the last family to live in the damned house. It burned to the ground — for the last time — in 1906.

THE NANNY

Windcrest, Nova Scotia

The 1830 farmhouse known as the old Hagen Place had an almost mystical pull on the middle-aged couple. When it came on the market finally, it was a foregone conclusion that they would buy it for a combination summer/retirement retreat. Little did they know that a ghost they came to call the "old lady" would also share their lives in the home they renamed Windcrest.

The couple's daughter, M.R. Mulvale, of Greenwood, Nova Scotia, said that her mother described "only half in jest" the ghost's activities over the years.

"As they drove away to the city after a weekend at Windcrest," M.R. said, "my mother regularly noticed the curtains move in the window of the only unused room upstairs. The house's door was routinely hooked shut [because the door latch was broken] before they left — and just as routinely was found unhooked upon their return the following Friday." No other signs of disturbance were ever found, nor was there evidence of a break-in by burglars.

"My father also accepted the old lady's residence, but he never gave specific details of any encounters. But whenever he couldn't find a particular tool, he was quick to implicate her and her 'borrowing' habits."

But an incident in 1970 involving M.R. and her two children convinced everyone that Windcrest did, indeed, harbour a mysterious spirit.

"Kate, who was three, had long conversations with who-knows-whom at bedtime as a matter of course," M.R. said. Neither mother nor grandparents paid much attention to the child's patter, assuming she could see someone they couldn't.

The other child was Terry, a very active three-month-old who, according to his mother, was "the world champion kicker-off of blankets in his age group." She said he would chatter at length while kicking off his blankets and falling asleep.

"One evening I went upstairs and tucked him in after he had thrashed himself to sleep. Sometime later, he awoke and repeated his bedtime performance — heard by four adults. I told my mother we would let him wear himself out."

Within a few minutes the thumps and bumps and wails from his crib ceased. Wanting to make sure that her son was all right, M.R. went upstairs to the bedroom and peeked inside.

"He was sound asleep," M.R. said, "and tucked in tightly. Unless he had been bellowing full tilt without moving a muscle, somebody had soothed him and tucked him in again."

And, she concludes, "It wasn't *any physical* being in the house." Even ghosts must have a hard time sleeping through a toddler's cries.

THE HAUNTED HILL

Siwash Hill, British Columbia

About midway up Vancouver Island, some 225 kilometres northwest of Victoria, are the communities of Courtenay and Comox. Courtenay is inland, but Comox lies right on the Strait of Georgia, directly across from Powell River, B.C., which can be reached by ferry from the island.

Today the two communities are placid island settlements with a combined population of about sixteen thousand. However, many years ago the area was visited by a female apparition that became the talk of the towns.

The ghost was described as a lanky woman, garbed in a brown cloak, with no arms or legs visible, only an indistinct blur. Her face was especially hideous — "nothing like a human face," one man who had seen her said — and marked by two deep black holes where the eyes should have been.

Siwash Hill, on the Comox-Courtenay Highway, was the place where local residents and even some tourists said they had seen her. The hill is some 185 metres from the sea. The speculation was that the ghost was somehow connected with an ancient battle that had taken place some 450 metres from the top of the hill between the Comox people and their enemies, the Haida Band, from the Queen Charlotte Islands. The Comox burial ground was at the bottom of the hill. It was from that direction that the ghost most often appeared.

The first verified sighting of the apparition came in mid-December 1940, when farmer William Day had an unnerving experience as he walked past the old burial ground. He was carrying a few groceries home when the bouncing shafts of light from his oil lantern fell upon a figure standing alongside the road about six metres in front of him. It quickly vanished and Day continued up the hill.

A few metres farther on, however, the figure reappeared almost directly in front of Day. It was a woman who appeared to be staring out toward the sea.

The woman slowly turned toward Day, and that's when he noticed her eyes. "They were piercing holes that seemed to look through me," he said. She had long, luxuriant hair that moved gently in the soft sea breezes.

Day thought someone was playing a trick on him. He disabused himself of that notion very quickly. "I have always laughed at ghosts and things of that kind, but I was in my sober senses, and I have told you exactly what happened," Day said.

A sailor returning to his ship one night saw *and* heard the ghost of Siwash Hill. "I saw a thing about halfway up the hill," he told reporters. He was so frightened that he ran all the way back to the harbour — and right off the end of Comox Wharf.

Construction projects also seemed to disturb the ghost. Whenever repairs or work projects were undertaken, drivers on the Comox-Courtenay Highway said they would see a woman standing in the roadway, directly in front of their cars. Unable to stop from hitting her in time, the drivers were astonished to see the figure vanish just before impact.

One of her last reported appearances came after a highway crew putting in a new water main alongside Siwash Hill stumbled upon a human skeleton. The next night the spectre was glimpsed hovering above the disturbed grave.

A POETIC DEATH

Bon Echo, Ontario

"The Good Grey Poet" is the lamentable nickname by which American poet Walt Whitman came to be called, erroneously suggesting a harmless, kindly old man when actually he was considered daring and even "immoral," particularly after the publication of the first edition of his famous *Leaves of Grass* in 1855.

Although it was not well received by critics upon publication, the initial collection of twelve untitled poems and his subsequent work catapulted Whitman into the front ranks of literary geniuses. Whitman, also an essayist and journalist, grew in popularity and stature so that upon his death in 1892, the man who had only a few years of schooling and had once toiled as a carpenter and contractor was known as the "bard of democracy." His verse commemorating the assassination of Abraham Lincoln, "O Captain! My Captain!", was memorized by generations of schoolchildren.

There is quite another reason Whitman occupies a niche in the annals of Canadian hauntings, however, one that has less connection to his poems and more to do with his personal character.

The poet's biographers have written extensively of his devotion to the wounded during the Civil War. When his brother came home a casualty in 1862, Whitman went to Washington to nurse him. He stayed on as a volunteer in army hospitals. Never one to let his experiences lie fallow, he wrote his impressions of the war and published these poems as *Drum-Taps* in 1865.

That theme of selflessness, of his devotion to comrades, was one of Whitman's primary traits. Is it any wonder then that Whitman's devotion to his close friends might transcend death?

That is exactly what several people say happened in the summer of 1919, nearly thirty years after the poet's passing at his home on Mickle Street in Camden, New Jersey.

The event that summer was peculiar in itself. It was the dedication of a peculiar crag on a bluff known as Bon Echo Rock, near the village of Bon Echo, Ontario, to the memory of Walt Whitman. The Rock itself is nearly 3 kilometres long and 120 metres high. Ancient Native Canadian paintings have been found on it, and a local legend holds that a treasure hides in a lost cave somewhere in the cliff.

The reason for its dedication to Whitman was that from certain directions and in certain lighting conditions, the crag was said to look like the head of an old man with whiskers. It was given the nickname "Old Walt," because some thought it resembled the poet; more pragmatic observers said it more closely paralleled the Egyptian Sphinx, if it looked like anything other than stone at all.

Several notables connected with Whitman came to

Bon Echo for the ceremonies, including Horace Traubel. He was one of the "band of disciples" who gathered at Whitman's New Jersey home during the final years of the poet's life. Traubel, whom some called Whitman's Boswell because he wrote several books about Whitman's life which he called the *Diary,* was one of the literary executors of his estate.

Traubel was very ill when he arrived in Bon Echo. A heart ailment had become acute; it was apparent that his last days might be spent in that Ontario hamlet.

Traubel's host in Bon Echo was Mrs. Flora MacDonald Denison, one of the leaders in the effort to dedicate the Bon Echo Rock crag in Whitman's honour. During Traubel's stay in her home, Mrs. Denison claimed that the spirit of Walt Whitman was at the dying man's side. Several other witnesses backed up her claim. The story was published in the local newspaper several years later, and signed affidavits were obtained from Mrs. Denison and others at the behest of the Society for Psychical Research.

At the end of August 1919, Traubel was so ill that he was confined to Mrs. Denison's home, moving only from his bedroom to the veranda, from which he had a picturesque view of "Old Walt." Traubel's wife, Anne, stayed at his side, relieved only occasionally by Mrs. Denison.

Traubel had been utterly depressed by his deteriorating health, but that changed on the evening of August 28. He had been sitting on the porch watching as twilight descended across the crag. As he was being assisted inside, he suddenly brightened and pointed into the distance.

"Look Flora! Quick, quick, he's going!"

Mrs. Denison turned but couldn't see anything. "What? Where, Horace?" she asked.

"Just over the rock. Walt was there, head and shoulders and with his hat on, brilliant and splendid. He beckoned to me, and spoke to me. I heard his voice, but I didn't understand all he said, only 'Come on!' "

Traubel's mood changed dramatically. He was cheerful, grateful for even the smallest of kindnesses from his many visitors, and confident in what he, alone, had seen. Mrs. Denison hadn't shared the vision, but she was able to see his disposition change. Sadly, his physical health continued to decline.

Over the next few days, he told Mrs. Denison that he heard Whitman's voice again urging him to "come on," and said that he saw visions of several of their mutual friends, including the politician and orator Robert Ingersoll. He smiled when he thought of Ingersoll in particular. It was he who had written to Whitman shortly before the latter's death: "May the Lord love you, but not too soon."

The visions of a dying man would have been dismissed as typical deathbed hallucinations were it not for the fact that the most dramatic incident — the actual appearance of the ghost of Walt Whitman — was witnessed by Traubel *and* Canadian army colonel L. Moore Cosgrove. Colonel Cosgrove wrote a detailed report for the American Society for Psychical Research the following year:

"During the months of August and September, 1919, I was in close touch with Mr. Horace Traubel, whom I had known through his numerous writings. I had not previously known him personally, nor had I a deep knowledge of the works and ideals of Walt Whitman. This I state to show that my mind, conscious or subconscious, was not subject to illusions concerning them."

Colonel Cosgrove noted that he had served in France during World War I and thus was familiar with death and the "atmosphere surrounding the dying." He was not particularly emotional during Traubel's final days, and he described the dying man as having thoughts that were "very clear," and said he was "without pain and seemed perfectly conscious."

The army colonel was with Traubel quite late one night a few days after he said Whitman had spoken to him:

"[Traubel's] eyes were closed and after some time he stirred restlessly, his eyes opened and he started as if to change to the other side of the bed. His lips moved as if he were trying to speak. I put back his head, thinking he needed more air, but he moved again and his eyes remained riveted on a spot some 3 feet above the bed. At last my own eyes were irresistibly drawn to the same point in the darkness — there was but a small, shaded light behind the curtain on the farther side of the room.

"Slowly, the point at which we were both looking grew gradually brighter, and then a light haze appeared. It spread until it assumed bodily form, and it had the likeness to Walt Whitman, standing beside the bed, a rough tweed jacket on, an old felt hat on his head and his right hand in his pocket. He was gazing down at Traubel, a kindly, reassuring smile on his face. He nodded twice as though reassuringly.

"Whitman . . . moved closer to Horace from the farther side of the bed. The strength of the dying man was ebbing and he was forced to allow his head to roll back.

"Suddenly [Horace] said, 'There is Walt!'

"As he said this the ghost passed, apparently through the bed and toward me, and appeared to touch my hand as though in farewell. I distinctly felt it, as though I'd had an electric charge. The figure gradually faded from sight."

Colonel Cosgrove said Traubel's features softened, almost as if the strain of dying had been lifted by the poet's startling deathbed appearance.

"I did not regard the event as extraordinary at the time," Colonel Cosgrove said. "I had experienced similar phenomena at crucial moments during heavy casualties in France."

Horace Traubel died two hours later.

A BROKEN PROMISE

Notre-Dame-de-Pontmain, Quebec

When the troubles began, Catherine Longpre was alone with her young son in her house by the river. Her husband, Georges Cloutier, was away working at a logging camp.

The horses wouldn't settle down when she tried to bring them in one evening. They shied away from her, jumping and bucking at her every approach. Exhausted, frustrated, and not a little mystified by her usually docile animals' tumultuous behaviour, Catherine paddled a small boat across the river to get help from her neighbour, Eva Duciaume.

The women finally succeeded in getting the horses corralled and went inside the Cloutiers' simple, rural home. Catherine sat down and lit a cigarette. As she snuffed out the match, her gaze shifted to the downstairs bedroom, which she could see through an open door. Her eyes widened. Stacked upon the bed was a pile of firewood normally kept by the stove. It was neatly placed, as if someone had mistaken the old bed with its feather mattress for the wood bin. Except no one other than Catherine and her young child, and now Eva, had been in the house all day. The wood hadn't been there an hour before.

Catherine told Eva that was it — she was truly frightened now and wasn't about to stay by herself in the house any longer.

Catherine Longpre and her husband Georges Cloutier had only one young son, Florian, in 1922, the year the puzzling incidents unfolded at their home not far from Notre-Dame-de-Pontmain in western Quebec.

During a period of several months in 1922, Georges and Catherine's home was possessed. The couple, along with several other witnesses, described a series of unimaginable events that seemed, for a time, to be without explanation.

The history of what happened to the couple and how the mystery was finally resolved by at last following a dying old woman's last request, is recounted by Clovis Daoust, who knew some of the people involved and now lives on land once occupied by the Cloutier cabin in rural Notre-Dame-de-Pontmain.

Eva Duciaume had to return to her own home that night, so Catherine hurried to the house of Leon Dicaire and his family. She asked if the boys, Hermas, who was nine, and eleven-year-old Joseph, could keep her company that night. She explained what had transpired and their parents agreed that the boys could help her keep "guard" overnight.

Some years later, Hermas recalled that it was one of the most amazing nights of his life. As he slept in his bed, he saw a rocking chair moving from side to side in the kitchen. Hermas woke up both his brother and Catherine, and they, too, saw the rocker move.

The next morning, Catherine told the boys she hadn't slept the entire night. For most of the time, she said, the flame of an oil lamp that had been left on moved up and down at regular intervals.

Over the next several days, various phenomena were sighted. A large, wet rock rolled noisily down the stairs. Hermas said it looked as if it had come from the river. Georges and Catherine's dog didn't budge, even though the rock landed near him. Later, two other rocks seemed to come from nowhere and collided in midair.

Catherine was nearly hysterical. She sent word to her husband about what was happening in the house and begged him to return from the camp as soon as possible. In the meantime, Catherine moved in with Leon Dicaire and his wife, Rose de Lima Valiquett, the parents of young Hermas and Joseph. The boys were too frightened to stay another night in Catherine's own cabin. They had never seen such things — shoes and baskets would dance about the rooms, an egg-basket slid across the floor, potatoes placed in a sack bounced back out.

Leon and Rose genuinely doubted Catherine's story and looked upon their sons' tales with amusement — until Leon saw with his own eyes one of the most incredible sights he had ever beheld.

On the day after Catherine moved in, she and the Dicaires had gone back to the vacant house to finish some chores. Shortly after noon, they suddenly noticed several pieces of laundry zoom out an open bedroom window, caper down the clothesline and "dance" toward the river. "They came back jumping as if somebody was inside," Hermas recalled. Skirts, stockings, shirts, and trousers bounced back across the ground, up the clothesline, and retreated through the window into the house.

To say the little group was astonished is an understatement. Leon checked all around the house but found no accounting for what had happened.

Later that night, Catherine and the Dicaires observed lights going on and off in various parts of the cabin, sometimes downstairs, then upstairs, and back down and so forth for several minutes at a time.

Georges Cloutier came home the next day from the camp near Carp's Creek, jesting that his wife was making up the whole story because she was jealous of the two young women cooking for the loggers. But when Leon told him what *he* had seen, Georges grew more serious.

He would soon see for himself that his wife and friends were not joking.

Leon Dicaire left to deliver some oxen he had sold to a man some kilometres away. Georges and the Dicaire boys spent the day cutting hay. While Catherine prepared supper that evening, Georges and his "apprentices" enjoyed a cold drink.

Catherine was turning a thick omelette when a loud crash came from the same downstairs bedroom in which she had earlier seen the stacked firewood. Georges rushed to open the door but found it partly blocked by one of the beds inside. He put his shoulder against the door and succeeded in opening it far enough so that he could peek inside — and cried out in astonishment.

The mattress was *floating* several feet above the bed!

The boys came running to the door and stared unbelievingly as the mattress rose to just below the ceiling, banked, and crossed the room.

Catherine grabbed her child and, with Georges and the stricken boys, ran out of the house and didn't stop until they had all reached the Dicaires'. Leon arrived home shortly thereafter. He went with Georges and another neighbour back to the house. They found the mattress slanted between the two beds in the room. It was stiff. When Leon tried to lift a corner of the mattress to put it back on the bed, it seemed to recoil "as if it had been attacked." Try as they might, the men could not get it out from between the beds.

They left for the night and returned the next day. The mattress was soft and malleable, and the men easily got it back on the bed.

Georges and Catherine had almost decided to move when someone suggested that perhaps the Church could help. Special masses might be said to relieve their home of whatever entity was plaguing it. This they tried, and the phenomena vanished for a time. The little family was allowed to live in peace.

What really happened in that house by the river?

The likeliest explanation of the phenomena was finally offered by Johnny Cloutier, Georges' elderly father. He had lived in the house before his son and daughter-in-law moved in.

He said, with some regret, that just before his wife, Julie, died in the house and in the bed in the downstairs bedroom, he had promised to have special masses said for her. He had not carried out his promise. Perhaps it was she who was calling attention to the broken pact by creating mischief in her old home.

Johnny also revealed that he often awoke at his new home in Pontmain with someone tugging on his hand. That, too, might have been Julie, he thought.

Georges had the masses said for his late mother and the phenomena disappeared while he lived there.

In later years there were other stories of that house —

of how one could see dancing couples through its windows, even though it was unoccupied and snow was piled halfway up the front door; of hot utensils that were sometimes found scattered over the kitchen floor; and of how the hand-wound wall clock was found working after an owner had been away for several months.

The house was torn down long ago, its materials used to build a barn and stables, and later Clovis Daoust's sturdy home. But the story of what happened in the old Longpre/Cloutier home remains as alive — and as mystifying — as if it were only yesterday.

THE PRESBYTERY

Tors Cove, Newfoundland and Labrador

Father Cody built the presbytery on the hill in Tors Cove, Newfoundland, over a hundred years ago. Locals called it "the palace," because the good minister used only the finest materials to build the house — ornate outside moldings, hand-carved woodwork, an angled staircase.

With so much attention to detail, is it extraordinary to learn that Father Cody never let go and continued to preside over his quarters?

The mystery of the presbytery begins when Cody still lived there. He was gone one weekend and his housekeeper invited a friend to stay over. The friend awoke at 3:45 the next morning after a dream in which her seafarer son had spoken to her, had in fact bid his mother goodbye. Father Cody's housekeeper learned a few days later that her friend received word that her son had drowned — at precisely the same time his mother had reportedly seen him in her dream.

More recently, a Newfoundland artist rented the "palace." He didn't know of its haunted history, but soon discovered for himself its peculiar qualities.

A kitchen door leading to a "mudroom" that separated the kitchen from the back door kept opening. Going out that way was also the quickest way to the church. Since he lived there alone, the artist blamed it on "the wind." One night while he was working at the kitchen table, however, the artist heard a noise behind him and turned to see the door opening as if to allow someone to enter.

He nailed the door shut. That worked for several months until he went away for a few days and returned to discover the nail on the floor and the door wide open.

Many people in Tors Cove wouldn't go near the presbytery, even during the day. Tradesmen were reluctant to provide repairs. A carpenter told the artist that he had been laying a new floor in the house when Father Cody "spoke" to him. He also saw someone going up the staircase, even though he was alone.

A plumber refused to shut off the water when the artist eventually moved out. The reputation of the presbytery on the hill was enough to keep him away.

DEATH BED

Vancouver, British Columbia

Will remodelling a house remove an "uncomfortable" feeling that may presage a haunting? Can a single, spectacular apparition exhaust a ghost's energy?

These are the interesting questions posed by a turn-of-the-century story from Vancouver's West End.

A middle-aged couple built their new house there but lived in it for only six months before the wife died. Her husband sold the place and moved from the city.

From the very beginning, the new owners were decidedly uncomfortable on the home's main floor, especially in the master bedroom. They decided that remodelling might help alleviate their anxiety. A small drawing room adjacent to the former master bedroom was enlarged to include the old bedroom, walls were moved, new rugs and furniture were purchased for every room, and the walls were refurbished.

It didn't work.

The couple held a party to celebrate the home's new look. Two women told newspaper columnist Harold Weir about the festivities — sixty years after the event. They had remained silent all those decades, and refused to give Weir even the names of the family involved. All the revellers had been pledged to secrecy.

"At precisely eleven o'clock, when all was going merrily," Weir wrote of the women's account, "the guests suddenly became conscious of something strange going on at the end of the drawing room where the bedroom had been. It was like a whirlwind of nothingness, sensed rather than seen.

"The room grew unaccountably cold and tongues were not so unaccountably silenced."

A four-poster rosewood bed emerged from the "whirlwind."

"A woman was lying [on the bed] clearly at the point of departure from this life," the women told Weir.

What truly frightened the assembled guests was that the woman was staring in wide-eyed horror at the indistinct figure of a man sitting in a Victorian chair near the bed. The astounding scene remained visible for some time and then faded away.

Everyone except the owners left, but not before they swore never to reveal what they had seen. Within a very short time the couple who had taken so much time and energy to "remodel the ghosts away" had sold the house and put all the furniture up for auction.

Weir said one of the women who had told him the story saved the strangest part for last. She told him she had later attended the auction of the owners' furniture.

Weir wrote:

"The new drawing room rug, where the phantom four-poster had rested, was marked by four well-worn indentations, exactly as though some heavy piece of furniture had rested there for a matter of months." Nothing was sitting in that position on the rug after the remodelling.

The house was eventually torn down, replaced by an anonymous, and presumably unhaunted, apartment building.

THE MILL

Manotick, Ontario

Anna Crosby Currier could not have been happier.

She had just returned to Manotick, Ontario, from a honeymoon in New York with her wealthy new husband, Joseph Merrill Currier. On this night in 1861 she held tight to her husband's arm as the couple proudly showed guests around the five-storey mill Joseph and his partner, shipping magnate Moss Kent Dickinson, had built on the Rideau River, south of Ottawa, the primary shipping lane between Ottawa and Kingston, Ontario.

Dickinson and Currier had spent lavishly to equip the mill. It had been originally built in 1860 to grind flour but was later expanded to house woollen and sawmills. Hand-carved woodwork could be found throughout the mill, the walls were plastered, and imported Buhrstone quartz from France was used for the millstones.

Currier had thrown himself into his new venture in part to help recover from the loss of three of his four children to scarlet fever and the subsequent death of his first wife, Christina.

Joseph Currier had asked Anna Crosby to marry him about a year after the mill opened. So it was that after the wedding and honeymoon, the couple had invited friends to join them at the mill for a reception and tour of what was then one of the most important businesses in northeastern Ontario.

Exquisite in a floor-length gown, Anna strolled through the mill at her husband's side, smiling delightedly as he pointed out the mill's costly details.

It was on the second floor that the unimaginable took place.

Large grain bins spread over the floor had forced the Curriers and their guests to split into several smaller parties. Somehow Anna got separated from the rest. Suddenly her long skirt became ensnared in one of the gears and she was yanked toward a large, spinning shaft. Her screams were drowned out by the pounding din of the grinders and the thundering water turbines. The shaft spun her about and heaved her against a wood beam, crushing her skull. That's where the revellers found her minutes later.

Moss Dickinson bought out the distraught Joseph Currier's shares and owned the mill for a number of years. Several owners ran the operation until 1972, when the Rideau Valley Conservation Authority bought what was by then called Watson's Mill. After fully restoring it, the Authority opened it for public tours in 1975.

Anna Crosby Currier became a highlight on some of the tours. Her *ghost*, that is.

There was that second-storey window from which a pale young woman sometimes stared. She would quickly duck away whenever someone gazed too long or too hard at her. Then she would resume her forlorn pacing on that floor, the same one on which she had been killed.

An official with the Authority said people usually saw Anna "on summer nights when the shadows are tall."

EMILY CARR

St. Ann's Academy, British Columbia

The old St. Ann's Academy was a girls' school and convent at one time. It was also the spectral home of eccentric Victoria artist Emily Carr . . . and maybe a few of her friends.

In 1991, retired businessman Arthur Knight told reporters he saw "twin ghosts" while he was out walking. "I was startled out of my wits . . . shaking like a leaf."

He described the figures as two women in hooded cloaks, one shiny white and the other grey, standing upon the front steps of St. Ann's. One woman was taller than the other. They disappeared at his approach.

He took several photos, one of which shows an indistinct shape in a window of the building. Another photo of the path and steps shows no footprints in the freshly fallen snow.

"Now, I'm not a religious person and I'm not a superstitious person, but I do believe in this phenomenon. I was really shaken," Knight told a reporter. He added that he didn't tell many people about his experiences. "I didn't do anything else because it sort of makes you seem silly."

At the time Knight saw the ghostly duo, a group called the Concerned Citizens Association was opposing a plan to turn St. Ann's into a tourist attraction. A spokesman for the group said many people had seen the ghost of artist Emily Carr there, but nothing else.

A local cable television producer wanted to interview Carr's ghost, especially after he too saw it.

"It was early evening," the man said, "and we were walking past St. Ann's. We looked up and saw a figure in one of the top windows . . . If she's trying to communicate, TV is a good medium."

There were no reports that Emily took him up on the offer.

THE GOOD DOCTOR

Sydney, Nova Scotia

The inexperienced may find it strange that real-life hauntings are quite often nothing to be feared. To many people, the knowledge that there is someone *unseen* with them while they go about their daily tasks is a comfort, and brings a peacefulness that is difficult to explain.

Such is the case with Miriam Siwak, of Sydney, Nova Scotia. She works for a stevedoring firm housed in an old building on the Government Wharf in that Cape Breton Island city. During World War II, the structure was used as a naval hospital. It's no wonder that an occasional apparition would make an appearance where life and death walked hand-in-hand.

"I have seen images in different sections of the building," Miriam began. "So many times that I no longer think it strange. But one night something different happened. I was working late and alone when I smelled pipe tobacco. Not smoke, but fresh tobacco. I thought nothing about it at first . . . but then it happened again. Not only does no one smoke in our office, but there hadn't been a pipe smoker in it for months."

The stevedore company has the only offices in the building, so Miriam doubted the tobacco smell could be coming from elsewhere. Later, Miriam related the incident to a friend. He reported back to her that his own father said the pipe smoke was probably coming from Doctor Stewart, a physician during the years the building had been a hospital. He was "always filling his pipe," Miriam was told. Although she hasn't been able to strictly confirm the identity of the doctor, Miriam points to several other incidents as proof that the good doctor, or someone, haunts the offices. She calls him — it? — her "friend."

"I was talking to my niece and the owner of the firm, Jim, when he asked me if there was anyone else in the building. I told him that there wasn't. He then said my 'friend' had just walked into my office! He described [what he had seen] as a silhouette in the shape of a man gliding into my office. That is exactly how I had described my 'friend' to other people after I had seen him."

The firm's secretary was working late one afternoon when she heard a man cough in one of the lower offices. She didn't think anything of it until she left her office a few minutes later. No one else was in the building. Who, then, coughed? Fearful of answering her own question, the secretary grabbed her coat and left.

One of Miriam's friends has had two unsettling experiences in the old building. Once he stopped in his office on Saturday morning to check for incoming faxes. He had his dog with him. "He was walking down the hall and his dog came up to the . . . washroom door and started to growl," Miriam recalled. "My friend knew someone was in the washroom and suspected a burglar. The dog growled steadily and all the hair stood up on her back. My friend went in to check and there was nothing to be seen. He closed the washroom door, but the dog stayed out there until he left the office. He knew there was something there, but only the dog could see it."

Several times Miriam's friend has heard file cabinet drawers opening and papers being shuffled noisily about in offices that are dark and locked.

Miriam Siwak is one of those witnesses to the supernatural who take the experience in stride.

"I know my friend is here. I feel he will always protect me. I don't fear being alone in the office; the only thing that frightens me when I work at night are the living who hang around the wharf area. If the spirit that occupies this office *were* evil I would have been gone long ago. I feel only peace when I work alone."

For that, Doctor Stewart — or whoever — deserves to be commended!

MYSTERY GHOST

New Westminster, British Columbia

The thirteen-room, turn-of-the-century Victorian mansion certainly *looked* like a haunted house. From its fish-scale wooden shingles and meandering porch, to the picket fence with old, wrought-iron hinges and heavy latches, the New Westminster home seemed pulled from a Charles Addams cartoon. Its situation on a dark, tree-shrouded avenue added to its gloomy bearing.

Looks are deceiving in this case. When the couple, with their three teenagers, bought the place in 1967, they knew that an extensive renovation was needed. A series of owners had left it in serious disrepair. The father was a carpenter and so he undertook a room-by-room facelift, taking down walls and doors, and building new rooms.

It wasn't until two years after the family moved in that their friend staying in a guest room saw the mysterious figure at the window. And even after he learned what happened, it was especially hard for the father to believe his "project" might be haunted. He was a person who believed there was an explanation for everything. His wife was more open-minded about the possibility of ghosts.

Later, other mysteries were added, including the sight of a female spectre gliding down the staircase. "The shadow of a woman," the mother told a reporter. "It was the only thing it could have been. She was wearing a long dress."

Then there were the times when one had the sense of someone being at one's side. Sometimes it happened on the couch while a family member watched television, a sensation that an invisible figure had sat down close by.

Late at night a kind of cold "whirlwind" enveloped the mother and followed her as she did housework.

Despite his avowal that events should be explainable, the father had his own shocks. The first occurred one night as he headed off to bed. He'd flipped off the downstairs lights and started up the stairs when "someone or something grabbed my hand." He said it was as if there was a person next to him holding his hand as he climbed the steps. He finally jerked his hand away, not quite knowing what to think.

There was a bathroom light that took a solid pull on the switch to turn it on. Family members downstairs would hear it click on and off — when no one was upstairs. Was there an explanation for the haunting?

A Vancouver psychic who visited the mansion "saw" an older man in an upstairs room standing over a washtub scrubbing clothes.

Shortly after the house was built, a family lived there who used to employ a Chinese man to wash clothes. Could that be who the psychic saw? Perhaps, he said, although the particular ghost he had seen might have been just "passing through" and not the resident haunt.

The psychic said there might be another candidate. He surprised the mother by detailing her family history, even stating accurately that her father's sister had died young. And, he added, her spirit now frequently visited the niece she never met in her mansion at New Westminster.

HEXED HOUSE

Keswick, Ontario

Sudden and unexpected changes in what one expects to find in a home one has lived in for some time can lead to the assumption that strange forces may be at work.

A family in Keswick, Ontario, had that discomforting thought in their fifty-year-old frame house. They called it an "evil spirit" and claimed it manifested itself in weird stains and peculiar bumps and rattles.

Keswick is about 80 kilometres north of Toronto on the southern end of Lake Simcoe. The family name was Matthews.

As reported in 1963, Mrs. Matthews said the "spirit" first appeared as a brown stain that looked like a skull and crossbones embedded in the kitchen floor. Another stain on a kitchen cabinet was the image of a woman in a hoop skirt.

Later, the cabinet doors swung open of their own accord, and dishes could be heard rattling day and night, almost as if a vibration undetected by the family rumbled through the house.

An occasional tapping at the front door was equally puzzling.

The family's attempt to get rid of the kitchen floor stain by holding a Bible over it just made the stain appear even brighter the next day.

In the end, Mrs. Matthews said, she just hoped the "spirit" would go away. It apparently did.

DISTURBED GRAVES

Coquitlam, British Columbia

Disturbing the dead can produce unforeseen consequences, as a young single mother discovered in Coquitlam.

One night in 1986, she reportedly saw the figure of a monk as she came out of the bathroom. She and her four children were out of the rented fourplex forthwith.

Tenants in the other units said unusual things happened to them, too — television channels switched unexpectedly and beds changed position.

It turns out the paving stones making up the fourplex's front walk were taken from one hundred and thirty graves at the Woodlands Hospital cemetery. Children's graves.

When the owner of the fourplex returned the stones, all was quiet once again.

THE WIDOW'S REVENGE

St. John's, Newfoundland and Labrador

The strangest house in the old city of St. John's, Newfoundland, was situated in the East End, before the calamitous fire of 1892 destroyed that neighbourhood. Well into the mid-twentieth century, however, many people were still alive who remembered the dreary house and the widow and her son who lived there. It was impossible to forget such a drab dwelling, and the chilling curse placed on its future tenants by the old woman.

A written description of the dwelling is all we have left as no photographs of it are known to exist. It was a house in perpetual darkness, with a narrow cornice and clapboard siding long unpainted; roofboards showed through where the shingles had rotted away. Yellowed shades covered dusty, perpetually unwashed windows that were never opened, though the shades were usually drawn up halfway each morning. The front door was flush with the street, but swung on rusty hinges each time it was opened.

The woman who lived in the house married late in life,

had a baby boy, and then watched as her husband died when the child was but an infant. She reared him as best she could, taking on menial housekeeping jobs or the washing and ironing for neighbours. As the boy grew he too took on his share of work, delivering newspapers or performing odd jobs around St. John's. Though his mother was illiterate, the boy finished enough school to read and do his figures.

St. John's in that era had a unique housing covenant. The custom of the period was to build houses on ground "leased" from landlords so that even though one owned the dwelling, rent had to be paid for the land upon which it had been built. This was the case with the widow and her son. Each year mother and son gathered enough money to pay their ground rent for the following year. In turn, the landlord gave them a receipt which the widow knew, even though she could neither read nor write, entitled them to continue living in the home in which she was raising her son. She carefully placed each year's receipt in a bureau drawer lest anyone challenge their occupancy.

In time the widow's son became a man. He decided that his mother had worked long enough and hard enough to support their meagre existence and now he would become the head of the house. He had no training for anything but humble labour, but that was plentiful in St. John's and provided enough income to put food on the table and simple clothes on their backs and pay the yearly ground rent. He followed his mother's custom in the latter task, delivering the rent to the landlord and requesting the receipt which he dutifully turned over to his mother.

The son fell in love. The young woman who became his bride agreed that she would move into the old house with her new husband and mother-in-law in order to save money. She was an expert decorator and soon the dreary house sparkled with new lace curtains and shades, freshly scrubbed floors and walls, and windows extricated from the accumulation of years of dust and grime. Even the hinges on the front door were oiled. A coat of "Dr. Bunting Green" paint was applied to the exterior. Never before had residents in St. John's East End seen such a glorious transformation.

But life for the widow, her son and his wife would not mirror the heartening changes in their home.

A baby was born to the son's wife. Now there were four mouths to feed, four persons to clothe, four persons who relied upon the son's slight income for all their worldly needs. And the baby, most especially, required a level of care that made the son's weekly pay sadly inadequate.

He thought long about the problem. At night he walked down to the harbour where he would sit on the pier and think through his alternatives. There were few.

He concluded that he had but one choice. He would put off paying the yearly ground rent for a few weeks, maybe a month or two at the most. That savings would give his baby extra food, perhaps his wife and his mother an item of clothing apiece, and the rest he would set aside to pay the landlord. It wouldn't take many weeks to make good on the rent, he reasoned, only long enough to get ahead a little bit. After all, what was more important, the landlord who had plenty of money or his own family with their meagre existence?

There was the problem of the receipt. His mother would expect the slip of paper after the yearly payment; he had carried on the custom over the years he had supported the household and had made sure his mother always got the receipt so she could put it away. He felt guilty about deceiving her, but what choice did he have? She would only see marks on the paper and assume they were in the landlord's handwriting. It was a small deception, he decided, although the guilt he felt over misleading her was great.

He found a sheet of white paper similar to the previous years' receipts and proudly gave it to her the year he decided to "delay" the ground rent. She smiled at her thoughtful son and placed it carefully in the bureau.

A few weeks passed and the son found that he still didn't have enough saved for the landlord, who didn't complain for he knew the family was honest. After six months, though, the son grew worried. His modest savings weren't nearly enough for the payment. He called upon the landlord with a story of an ill mother, a sickly child, and unexpected expenses, none of which was true but which trickery the son excused as necessary.

"During all the years since your father took out the lease," the understanding landlord said, "every payment but this one has been met on time, and I can understand how it is with you. If everybody paid up as well as your father, your mother, and yourself have done, there would be small cause to worry over bad bills."

Even a deception based upon the best motives can lead to tragic consequences. So it was with this family. Several years passed and each year the son put off his ground rent, being always careful to forge a receipt for his mother. The landlord, who was at first caring and understanding, grew impatient. He demanded payment in full. When the son confessed that he could not oblige, the landlord foreclosed on the house.

The widow wept on the day she was forced from the

home in which she had lived most of her life. Her son was to blame, in her heart she knew that, but as with many mothers she refused to think ill of her child. Instead, she cursed the landlord for the indignity of being tossed out of their home.

The family had no choice but to move into a tenement apartment which, it so happened, was just around the block from their home. Even the backyards adjoined and a window in the apartment looked out at their old house.

Since he didn't want the house to sit empty for too long, the landlord placed it on the market. It was all too much for the widow, who sat each day at the dingy tenement's back window, crying over the loss and screaming at anyone who seemed to be looking over the property.

Nearly everyone in the neighbourhood learned of the widow's plight, and watched as she kept vigil at the window. Potential buyers of her home were scared off by her angry imprecations that should they buy the house a curse would fall upon them and their families.

A prominent St. John's business owner scorned the idea of an old woman's curse. He was without superstition, the house was in adequate condition, and thus he could find no logical reason not to buy it.

On an evening after he'd made arrangements with the landlord to buy the new property, the businessman was sitting at his home when a knock came at the door. He opened it to find the old widow kneeling at the threshold, her hands clasped beseechingly before him.

"Please, sir, I beg of you not to buy the only home my son has ever known and the one in which I have lived my life," she wailed. "I know that you are a kind man at heart and would not trample upon an old woman's last wishes. I will pray for you every day and ask God to bring you and your family good fortune if you would only do as I ask."

In her delusional mind, the widow thought that if the house remained vacant the landlord would relent and allow her family to move back in. *He* was to blame! *He* was the one who had tossed them out on the street! She still believed her son deserved no culpability in the matter.

"I am sorry, my dear woman," the businessman replied. "It is unfortunate that you lost your home, but that is none of my concern. I paid a fair price for the property and intend to move in with my own family as soon as needed repairs can be made. I'm sure you will understand that it's just business. Nothing personal."

With that he closed the door. The old woman's tears stained her shawl as she pulled herself to her feet and turned to leave. Through narrow, reddened eyes, she glanced back at the door. He had not heard the last from her, she promised.

The businessman hired carpenters to repair his new house's roof and siding, painters to give it a fresh coat of paint, and handymen to replace the old windows with modern sashes. Light, diaphanous curtains allowed sunlight to penetrate the dark rooms for the first time in many years.

All the while, the old widow sat at the window of her tiny apartment watching the activity at "her" house. Though her health was rapidly failing, she was vitriolic in her denunciation of this man who "has taken the roof from above my head."

Soon the house was in readiness. The businessman, his wife, and two bright, vivacious teenage daughters — ages seventeen and fifteen — were thrilled with the remodelling and thought this would be just the place to spend the rest of their lives.

The yard had not been kept up for a very long time and after the remodelling was completed had become the family's main chore. Planting flower beds, a vegetable garden, and new grass took up most of their free time.

Shortly after his family moved in, the father was clearing an area in the backyard quite close to the picket fence that divided the property from the tenement in which the widow and her family lived. He often saw her sitting at the window, muttering to herself and cursing her ill fortune, but did his best to ignore her.

On this day she was again at the window. He wasn't looking her way when he heard her voice rising to a pitch he had never heard before. When he looked up he saw that she had thrown open the window and was leaning out in his direction, shaking her wrinkled fist at him.

"My curse upon you, you robber of the widow's mite," she screamed. "May your life be blasted and may the brightest flower of your family soon fade and perish."

With that she fell back from the window. The businessman was afraid she had collapsed and ran to a neighbour's door. He explained what he had seen (but kept to himself what she had said) and asked the neighbour to check on the old woman. He explained that it was probably best for him not to go himself to her apartment.

The widow had collapsed unconscious on the floor. She was taken to her bed, and there she remained for the final days of her life.

"I'll haunt him! I'll haunt him! My curse upon him!" she muttered over and over again as she lay in bed.

Her priest, neighbours, and even her son and daughter-in-law tried to persuade her not to depart with a curse against the businessman and his family upon her lips. She ignored them.

Then one night she clasped a neighbour woman's hand and said, "I'm nearing the end. I can feel myself slipping away."

"God is good and we must always hope for the best," the woman friend whispered, leaning close. "If you should die tonight, you would not want to enter the world beyond the grave with a curse upon your conscience."

The old woman nodded.

"And so you won't haunt him?" the friend asked.

"I will! I will haunt him for all eternity!" the old widow screeched, and fell back against her pillows. She died without saying another word.

A few days later the businessman was asleep in his bed when he suddenly sat bolt upright. Still groggy from sleep, he was vaguely aware of a distant, tolling bell — one . . . two . . . three times it chimed. He was frightened. Something within him said these were familiar sounds, yet he could not focus his consciousness on their source. His brain was still too clouded from sleep, but he had to know — where had he heard them before?

He lifted himself slowly to a sitting position at the edge of the bed and felt the soft, cool evening breeze drift in through the open window. Of course, the bells were from the old town clock! It could not possibly be as late as 3 o'clock in the morning; surely he must have slept through the first nine chimes and only become conscious of the final three strokes.

He got to his feet and tiptoed to the window, which looked out over the backyard. The moist air felt good upon his face as he leaned out and gazed into the night.

And then he felt his legs go weak and his heart started pounding so that he thought his chest would explode.

He gripped the window ledge and stared transfixed across the yard at the widow's apartment . . . and into the dead woman's face! She was at the window where she had sat vigil for so many months, shaking a bony finger at him. A pale light seemed to surround her.

He leaped back into his own bed and pulled the covers over his head, shaking and moaning so that his wife was roused from her sleep.

"Wake up, Jim! You're having a nightmare," she scolded.

He did not respond, but continued to burrow into the bedclothes as if he could escape the horrible sight so easily.

"Jim! Jim! Wake up, poor man," his wife cried. He grew quiet and finally sat up.

"I must have been dreaming," he said, not daring to speak to his wife of what he had seen for fear she would think him crazy.

"What time is it?" he asked.

"It must be after midnight," his wife assured him. "You're all nerved up. You must have had a very upsetting dream. Lie down and think of pleasant things before you go back to sleep."

"But I don't think I was dreaming . . . all of it," he insisted. "I'm sure I was awake and heard the town clock striking. I must see what time it is."

He struck a match, and in its flickering glow saw that the small clock on the bedstand showed one minute past midnight.

Nothing more was said of the incident. Whether it had all been a dream or whether he had seen the ghost of the dead woman gnawed at his brain, but he could neither resolve the dilemma nor escape the fear its continual presence in his thoughts brought to even the most mundane of daily tasks.

All was quiet for some time until an evening several weeks later. The wife was alone. Her husband was away on a business trip and their daughters were visiting schoolmates.

She was sitting in the kitchen with a collection of mending on her lap. The evening was rapidly shifting from daylight to darkness, and in the twilight she had lighted an oil lamp to help her see her sewing needles and thread.

A gust of wind abruptly swept through the room, extinguishing the lamp. A chill went down the wife's spine at the suddenness with which heavy dusk settled in the room. She had not entirely believed her husband's explanation on that earlier night that he had simply had a nightmare. And, too, she had learned about the old woman's supposed curse.

As she reached for a match with which to relight the lamp wick, the deep silence was broken by three sharp, distinct raps that resounded throughout the house, yet seemed to emanate from no one place in particular. She jumped at the unexpected sound. Carefully setting the sewing on the kitchen table, she got up to see if someone had come in through the front door.

She froze as she peered through the kitchen doorway. Standing inside the front entrance was a small, old woman with a shawl covering her shoulders and drawn up to obstruct most of her face. With an outstretched hand, the hag started shuffling down the hallway toward the doorway in which the terrified homemaker stood.

With a scream, the wife fell back into the kitchen and collapsed.

The next thing she knew, soft voices were urging her

to awaken. She opened her eyes to see her daughters and a neighbour leaning over her. She was in her own bed, warm blankets pulled up to her chin.

"Wasn't it all dark?" she asked.

"Yes, that it was," said the neighbour. "I heard you scream and came rushing over. I found you there on the floor of the kitchen and not a lamp lit in the entire house. And the front door was wide open. Seems to me the wind blew out the kitchen lamp. The chimney was still hot."

"Did . . . did . . . you see anyone?" the wife stammered, still very agitated from the events.

"Nobody," the neighbour said. "Well, nobody but an old beggar woman limping down the street." The girls added that they too had seen a stranger some distance from the house.

"Oh, I was terribly scared," the mother said. "The draft must have blown out the light — and then the beggar woman suddenly coming into the hall . . . at least I think it was a — " She broke off her final words, not daring to think about who else it might have been.

All of these elements must have combined at the right moment to produce this weird effect, the mother reasoned. The wind gust must have blown open the front door and then put out the lamp at the same moment the beggar woman rapped. Yet that wind was so cold as it came down the hallway ahead of the stranger . . . so cold that it seemed to penetrate to her very bones.

There was nothing conclusive in these two incidents to suggest that the widow's curse had taken hold of the businessman's family. Each might have been attributed to simple coincidence were it not for what happened on an exquisite late Newfoundland spring night several months later.

A thin strand of daylight remained on the western horizon as the deep blue sky darkened on its journey toward night. A sprinkling of stars twinkled their greetings to the shadows that fell softly over St. John's. Boats in the harbour swayed gently at their moorings. The world seemed a warm and generous place.

On that street and in that house where the widow once lived, the dinner hour had passed as pleasantly as usual. Father and mother had retired to the parlour, he to finish some paperwork and she to resume some intricate crocheting. The younger daughter was in her upstairs bedroom overlooking the street. The older daughter, the blooming rose of her father's eye, sat by the window in her room using the fading daylight to finish a piece of embroidery.

The soft air coming through the open window nudged the lace curtains aside and blew softly across the girl's face. She let the embroidery drop to her lap as she leaned back in the soft chair cushions. Her eyes closed. She let her mind wander among the million thoughts that young girls everywhere have at that age.

Minutes drifted by. The room settled into darkness. Suddenly the girl, who had been wandering among the stars, felt a slight chill. She opened her eyes. From where she sat there was a clear view across the backyards. At first there was only darkness at the dead widow's apartment, but gradually a pinpoint of light appeared in the one window where the woman had sat screeching her disgust to the girl's family. The light grew in intensity and in its glow the girl saw the old widow sitting in her chair at the window, but this time she was a corpse in a torn dress and ragged shawl. She raised her arm and pointed a bony finger toward the young girl.

The light, growing in intensity about the spectre, became like a shaft of rays spilling out across the yards, up the side of the girl's home and finally through her window and into her room, where she felt ensnared by its intensity.

As the beacon stretched between the two windows, the widow's ghost glided out her window, along the path of light, and hovered outside the girl's window. She rested her rotting arms on the sill and raised her grisly face. Shreds of flesh hung like streamers from her skull; where the eyes and nose should have been there were only dank holes. She stared through the window, her mouth pulled back in a hideous, toothless grin. She reached toward the girl.

The scream brought the girl's parents rushing into the bedroom. They found their daughter writhing on the floor, hysterical. She was crying, and speaking gibberish about lights and faces and old women, but completely unable to make any sense to her tormented parents.

A doctor came the next day and diagnosed the condition as "paralytic epilepsy" brought on by some sort of shock. He gave her medicine, and even brought in several colleagues to help in the diagnosis, but it was all to no avail.

The girl grew weaker with each passing day, unable to eat or to communicate with those around her. The doctor surmised that her brain had suffered such trauma from whatever event transpired that night that she was lost forever.

And in that condition this girl, this burnished flower in her parents' garden, passed from the earth. The widow's curse had triumphed.

BIBLIOGRAPHY

BOOKS

Beck, Horace. *Folklore and the Sea.* New York: Stephen
    Greene Press, 1973.

Blundell, Nigel, and Roger Boar. *The World's Greatest Ghosts.*
    New York: Berkeley, 1988.

Clarke, Ida Clyde. *Men Who Wouldn't Stay Dead.* n.p., n.d.

Creighton, Helen. *Bluenose Ghosts.* Toronto: McGraw-Hill
    Ryerson Limited, 1957.

Fink-Cline, Beverly, and Leigh Cline. *The Terrific Toronto Trivia
    Book.* Toronto: Personal Library Publishers, 1979.

Guiley, Rosemary. *Encyclopedia of Ghosts and Spirits.* New
    York: Facts on File, 1992.

Haining, Peter. *A Dictionary of Ghosts.* New York: Dorset
    Press, 1993.

Henningar, Ted R. *Scotian Spooks: Mystery and Violence.*
    Hantsport, N.S.: Lancelot Press, 1978.

Kevan, Martin. *The Best of Montreal and Quebec City.* New
    York: Crown, 1992.

Mosher, Edith. Haunted: *Tales of the Unexplained.* Hantsport,
    N.S.: Lancelot Press, 1982.

————. *The Sea and the Supernatural.* Hantsport, N.S.:
    Lancelot Press, 1974.

Notre-Dame-de-Pontmain, 1884–1984. n.d. (translated by
Anthony Baechle for the authors).

Russell, Paul and Jeffrey Robert. *Toronto's Top 10*. Toronto:
Methuen, 1984.

Sherwood, Roland H. *Maritime Mysteries*. Windsor, N.S.:
Lancelot Press, 1976.

————. *The Phantom Ship*. Hantsport, N.S.: Lancelot Press,
1975.

Singer, Kurt, ed. *The Unearthly*. New York: Belmont Books,
1965.

Smith, Susy. *Haunted Houses for the Millions*. New York:
Dell, 1967.

Sonin, Eileen. *ESP-ecially Ghosts*. Toronto: Clarke, Irwin and
Company, 1970.

Watson, Julie. *Ghost Stories and Legends of Prince Edward
Island*. Willowdale, Ont.: Hounslow Press, 1988.

PERIODICALS

Armstrong, John. "The Gallery of Ghosts: The eerie and
unexplained in old Burnaby mansion." *Vancouver Sun*,
October 31, 1987.

————. "Ghost eludes our intrepid reporter." *Vancouver Sun*,
October 31, 1987.

Bolan, Kim. "The haunted gallery." *Vancouver Sun*, October
31, 1986.

Bon Echo (Ont.) *Sunset*, May 17, 1928.

Carr, Tony. "Goodnight, Ghost." *Vancouver Sun*, December 9,
1977.

Caylor, Ron. "Priest Haunts Church." *National Enquirer*,
January 31, 1978.

Clark, Victor. "Metro's Ghostliest Places." *The Subway Link*,
vol. 1, no. 2 (October 31–November 20, 1986).

Clough, Peter. "Daily Planet." *Vancouver Province*, June 11,
1992.

Cobb, Michael. "She's Hostess With Ghostess." *Vancouver
Sun*, May 30, 1966.

"Courtenay Man Insists Ghost Woman Danced Right at Him." *Canadian Press*, ca. 1940.

Curtin, Fred. "Ghosts back at old haunts." *Vancouver Province*, April 9, 1964.

"Emily Carr Haunts Halls." *Vancouver Province*, May 12, 1991.

"Escape in a haunted house." n.p., n.s. June 17, 1966.

"Evil Spirit Hits House in Ontario." *Canadian Press*, June 12, 1963.

Fitzhenry, Jack. "The Widow's Curse." *The Newfoundland Quarterly*, December 1945.

Fralic, Shelley. "A ghost that stayed away." *Vancouver Sun*, November 1, 1982.

"Ghost Fee Ruled Out." *Vancouver Sun*, July 21, 1966.

"Ghostly Guests at Beckley Farm." n.s., May 8, 1955.

"Ghostly Presences Aid Atmosphere." *Vancouver Province*, n.d.

"Ghosts host haunted." *Vancouver Province*, June 24, 1966.

"Haunted house sold." *Vancouver Sun*, April 2, 1973.

Herman, Wendy. "Ghost town Toronto." *Toronto Star*, April 27, 1980.

Jamieson, Charles. "Are There Such Things as 'Tokens'?" *The Newfoundland Quarterly*, December 1928.

————. "The Ghostly Light Off Come-By-Chance Point." *The Newfoundland Quarterly*, October 1928.

"Jim Curran's Ghost." *Commercial Annual Christmas Number*, 1921, n.p.

Johnson, Eve. "So you don't believe in ghosts? Prepare yourselves for a shock." *Vancouver Sun*, October 30, 1981.

Marshall, Roger. "Dead builder 'walked' doomed Raven's decks." *Vancouver Province*, February 10, 1972.

Mills, Philip. "Mother, son share house with ghost." *Vancouver Province*, December 22, 1976.

"Motorists Report Strange Happenings on Highway." n.s., April 12, 1960.

"Mystery Knocks Alarm." *Canadian Press*, October 13, 1933.

"Night in a Haunted Home Long." *Vancouver Province*, May 15, 1950.

"Not a Chance," *Vancouver Province*, July 20, 1966.

Oberlyn, Ros. "Spook-hunters seem to be having a wail of a time." *Vancouver Sun*, October 24, 1978.

Odam, Jess. "Hefty's Haunted by Ghost Fans." *Vancouver Sun*, June 8, 1966.

————. "Sun Team Sees No Ghost — But What Was That in Hall?" *Vancouver Sun*, June 2, 1966.

"OOOOOOOOOHH, Ghostly Tales." *Vancouver Province*, May 12, 1991.

Rimes, Les. "Sun Man Sleeps on as 'Ghost' Gives Fiddle Solo." *The Island*, September 24, 1959.

"Scare Still On." *Vancouver Sun*, June 1, 1966.

Schaefer, Glen. "Our Scariest Haunts." *Vancouver Province*, October 28, 1990.

"The Schooner 'Isle of Skye.'" *Commercial Annual Christmas Number*, 1921, n.p.

Senn, Roma. "Things that go bump in the night." *Atlantic Insight*, October 1983.

Shortis, H. F. "Ghost Stories." *The Evening Telegram* (St. John's, Newfoundland), December 15, 1928.

"Spooky Trouble at mill." *Canadian Press*, March 9, 1985.

Stockand, Dave. "B.C. has its fair share of spooks." *Vancouver Sun*, October 29, 1977.

Stroud, Carstens. "The Case of the Missing Snipe." *Toronto Star*, December 9, 1979.

"Sunday Séance Seeks Shy Spook." *Vancouver Sun*, June 3, 1966.

"Two visits by 'phantom' tied to wall's tombstone." *Vancouver Sun*, October 26, 1982.

Volgenau, Gerald. "Ghostbusters: Pair Claims to Banish Spirit From Home." *Montreal Free Press*, n.d.

Weir, Harold. "Ghostly Secret." *Vancouver Sun*, November 2, 1961.

White, Scott. "Legislature's Past Spooky." *Vancouver Sun*, July 5, 1984.

"Who Wants Haunted House?" *Vancouver Province*, March 31, 1973.

UNPUBLISHED WORKS

Correspondence from Pierrette Champoux, Montreal, November–December, 1993.

Correspondence from Jocelyne Choquette, Montreal, December 1993. (translated by Anthony Baechle).

Correspondence from Judy Curry, Metropolitan Toronto Library Board, November 1986.

Correspondence from Clovis Daoust, Notre-Dame-de-Pontmain, Quebec, December 1993. (translated by Anthony Baechle)

Correspondence from Mrs. E. M. Darke, curatorial assistant for historic houses, Toronto Historical Board, January 1987.

Correspondence from Marie V. Gibbs, Moose Jaw, Saskatchewan, October 1993.

Correspondence from Jennifer Harrand, secretary, Burnaby Art Gallery, November 1994.

Correspondence from Laura Jantek, coordinator of reference services, Halifax City Regional Library, n.d.

Correspondence from Jean Moore, Regina, Saskatchewan, n.d.

Correspondence from M. R. Mulvale, Greenwood, Nova Scotia, December 1993.

Correspondence from Miriam Siwak, Sydney, Nova Scotia, October 1993.

Interview with Roy Bauer, Winnipeg, Manitoba, February 1994.